WITH
NAPOLEON'S
GUARD IN RUSSIA

WITH
NAPOLEON'S
GUARD IN RUSSIA

The Memoirs of Major Vionnet, 1812

Louis Joseph Vionnet

Translated and edited by
Jonathan North

Pen & Sword
MILITARY

First published in Great Britain in 2012 by
PEN & SWORD MILITARY
an imprint of
Pen & Sword Books Ltd
47 Church Street
Barnsley
South Yorkshire
S70 2AS

ISBN 978 1 84884 635 7

A CIP catalogue record for this book is
available from the British Library

Typeset in Ehrhardt
by L S Menzies-Earl

Printed and bound in England
by CPI Group (UK) Ltd, Croydon, CR0 4YY

Pen & Sword Books Ltd incorporates the imprints of
Pen & Sword Aviation, Pen & Sword Family History, Pen & Sword Maritime,
Pen & Sword Military, Pen & Sword Discovery, Wharncliffe Local History,
Wharncliffe True Crime, Wharncliffe Transport, Pen & Sword Select,
Pen & Sword Military Classics, Leo Cooper, Remember When,
The Praetorian Press, Seaforth Publishing and Frontline Publishing

For a complete list of Pen & Sword titles please contact
PEN & SWORD BOOKS LIMITED
47 Church Street, Barnsley, South Yorkshire, S70 2AS England
E-mail: enquiries@pen-and-sword.co.uk
Website: www.pen-and-sword.co.uk

Contents

List of Illustrations

List of Maps

Acknowledgements

Thanks are due to the very professional team at Pen and Sword, particularly to Rupert Harding for his unswerving support, and to the book's editor, Sarah Cook.

I would also like to thank Steven H. Smith, Ned Zuparko, Alain Le Coz (for his superb work on the Fusiliers-Grenadiers), Alexander Mikaberidze, Bas de Groot, Oscar Lopez, Evan Donevich, Jack Gill, Terry Doherty, Christophe Bourachot, Thomas Hemmann, Eman Vovsi, Digby Smith, Kevin Kiley, Paul Dawson and Dominique Laude. I am also grateful to the staff at the Bibliothèque nationale de France and to Chantal Prévot at the library of the Fondation Napoléon in Paris.

Whenever embarking upon a prolonged period of writing and research, the support of family is crucial. I feel especially lucky in this regard, and am grateful to my parents for tolerating that episode in 1982, and to Evgenia and Alexander without whom, as the saying goes, I would have finished this in half the time.

Note on the Text

Vionnet and his contemporaries were rather cavalier about spelling. Perhaps this was inevitable when France itself was a muddle of dialects and a confusion of patois. A survey from 1794 showed that six million French citizens were completely ignorant of French, and a further six million could barely converse in the language. For instance, when a French department was created out of a part of the Austrian Netherlands, it was given the name Jemmapes, simply a misspelling of the town of Jumape (now part of Mons in Belgium). Further confusion was then caused by changing the name to Jemappes. So perhaps it is understandable that if our protagonists could hardly agree on how to spell the names of French towns, then they would find it hard to agree on how to write those of remote villages in western Lithuania.

I have tried to use the place names generally agreed upon in the early nineteenth century so that this text can be read with and against other memoirs. So I have opted for Vilna, but adding the modern name Vilnius on first instance, rather than Wilna or Wilno. It has not always been possible to identify some locations, especially those in eastern Prussia or Silesia (territories which became Polish or Russian after 1945).

Similar problems bedevil individuals mentioned in the text. Vionnet is relatively good at accurately citing his comrades, but Sergeant Bourgogne, who fought in the same unit, is less reliable (possibly because he wrote his memoirs from memory while a prisoner of war). So Bourgogne cites Sergeant Leboude or Sergeant Oudicte when he means Jean-François-Nicolas Leboutte or Sergeant-Major Nicolas Oudiette. Bourgogne is an interesting example. He did at least get Lieutenant Serraris's name right, but his English translator muddled it into the beautiful but incorrect Lieutenant Cesarisse, something which also happened to Joseph Vachin (who inexplicably became Captain Vachain).

All translations are my own. I have been fortunate to have had available both editions of Vionnet's text (the 1899 edition and the 1913 edition). The earlier edition includes some text from the very opening of the Russian campaign, which the 1913 edition omits, but both conclude at the same point in time. I have preferred to translate Bourgogne's memoirs from the French, not only because of the reasons stated above, but also because the English edition misses out some important details and omits entire paragraphs that can be found in the French text.

This book is very much the story of Major Vionnet, of his comrades in arms and of the regiment in which he so proudly fought. It focuses on the 1812 campaign in Russia, and on the disaster that befell Napoleon's armies in that terrible year. Vionnet's own account of the debacle is supplemented by accounts of those who fought alongside him. Perhaps because Vionnet's unit, the Fusiliers-Grenadiers of the Imperial Guard, insisted on recruiting amongst the literate, we have been fortunate enough to be able to make use of surviving texts by Lieutenant Serraris, Lieutenant Vachin, Sergeant Bourgogne, Sergeant Scheltens, Corporal Michaud and, for early 1813, Surgeon Lagneau. I have also added in some text from the man who commanded Vionnet's division, the rather unsympathetic General Roguet. All these men served with this regiment, and their accounts supplement or confirm Vionnet's own account. It makes for a useful corroboration of facts, and can sometimes prove amusing. For example, we have Vionnet and Roguet fulminating against pillagers and looters (blaming foreigners, or thieves), while their NCOs cheerfully describe how much pillaging they have been doing, how much money they have accrued and what supplies they have obtained (to share occasionally with their officers).

I have, it might seem arbitrarily, concluded Vionnet's account after he was wounded in 1813, a few months after he was transferred out of the Fusiliers-Grenadiers. It seemed a logical point at which to curtail the story of the Russian campaign, and it goes to show that few of those who survived that catastrophe remained unscathed in the disaster in Germany in 1813.

Introduction

Vionnet and his Regiment

Napoleon's Imperial Guard was a vital part of the armies that conquered much of Europe. It was an organisation on which he lavished a sustained degree of meticulous Napoleonic attention, from matters of personnel, dress, deportment and pay, to deployment on the battlefield.

The Guard had originated from bodies of reliable troops hand-picked to guard the National Assembly in 1789, to offset the gathering storms in a turbulent Paris. By late 1795, after various changes of name, purges and reorganisations, a unit of horse and foot named the Garde du Directoire emerged to protect the Directory as it went about its business. It was composed of veterans, formed into infantry (not yet sporting the famous bearskins) and cavalry (chiefly based on personnel from the 3rd Dragoons) and had a band of brilliant musicians attached. Napoleon's coup in November 1799 allowed him a free hand to fashion his own household troops. Using the Garde du Directoire as a base, he merged it with other guard units, filled it with loyal supporters and expanded it to become two battalions of Grenadiers (now in tall bearskins) and a company of Chasseurs à Pied, as well as some mounted chasseurs (Chasseurs à Cheval) and a squadron of mounted Grenadiers. Some artillery was also attached. From this nucleus the Guard began to grow and to establish itself as an army within an army, especially when Napoleon proclaimed himself Consul for life and gave himself a free hand to do as he pleased in all matters of state. He sought to place reliable veterans in the Guard, literate men no younger than twenty-five years of age who had already served in three campaigns (ideally including those led by Napoleon himself). In return the men enjoyed enhanced status and enhanced pay (450 francs a year for a Grenadier). In 1800, as Napoleon sought to sweep the Allies once more from the plains of Italy, the Guard earned its preferential treatment by playing an important part in the victory at Marengo, and paid for it with heavy losses. It was then to be increased still further in November 1801, recruiting men from the line (now required to have served in four campaigns) who were at least 1.80 metres tall if they wanted to be a Grenadier or 1.70 metres if they wished to become a Chasseur.

The Guard was not the only elite unit in the French Army: the line regiments had their companies of grenadiers, the light had their carabiniers. But the Guard, from the point of view of prestige, and as a career, was pre-eminent. Especially when, in July 1804, it became the Imperial Guard, following Napoleon's own self-promotion. The Guard now boasted a complement of 9,000 men, and included the famous Mamelukes, as well as a battalion of sailors, and each Guard infantry regiment had a battalion of velites attached. These were promising recruits, some volunteers, some well-bred conscripts, who were destined to serve such an apprenticeship before becoming fully fledged Guardsmen or NCOs or officers in the line.

Formation

In April 1806, following the successful conclusion of his campaign against the Austrians and Russians at Austerlitz, where the Imperial Guard met Czar Alexander's Guard, Napoleon increased his Guard still further. He found that having velites was an expensive way of training future personnel for the Guard, and by the autumn of 1806 was looking to establish a regiment of Fusiliers. These would be young recruits, again destined for great things but also marked down for a much more active role on the battlefield than the elite Grenadier and Chasseur regiments. Napoleon wanted them to cost less than the Guard, but be better off than men in the line units (pay was fixed at 2.66 francs a day for sergeant-majors, 2.22 for sergeants, 1.66 for corporals, 0.60 for Fusiliers and 1.38 for drummers; by contrast, a grenadier in a line regiment had to make do with 0.30 francs). The regiment would have a uniform which would reflect the status of the Guard's 'finishing school', and the men would wear their hair powdered and in a queue, but they would have a shako, like their line brethren, rather than a bearskin. The shako was useful; it offered some protection and Scheltens kept his notebook in it as well as a purse with coins. This compromise in dress and status would lead to such units being called the Middle Guard. The officers would largely be drawn from the velites, bolstered by some from the Grenadiers. In December 1806 the establishment of a single regiment of Fusiliers was overturned and it was decreed that there should in fact be two regiments: the 1st Regiment, attached to the Chasseurs, and soon to be known as the Fusiliers-Chasseurs; and the 2nd Regiment, attached to the Grenadiers, and known as the Fusiliers-Grenadiers (or, on occasion, the Fusiliers of the 2nd Regiment of Grenadiers, but this was found to be confusing). The two regiments were brigaded together. Recruits (who had to be more than 1.73 metres tall) were sought and the supply of arms, equipment and uniforms was contracted. Just before Christmas 1806 the first recruits, men such as Jean Arent and Pierre Laux (both of whom were later promoted into the Grenadiers of the Guard, and both of whom disappeared in Russia in 1812), began to arrive at the Fusiliers-Grenadiers' depot (shared with the Grenadiers) at Courbevoie in the north-westerly outskirts of Paris. They were donning their new uniforms when, in January 1807, the regiment received news that its first colonel, the comparatively young (33) and modestly named Jean Parfait Friederichs, had been appointed. He had been a soldier since the age of 16; before his transfer to the Fusiliers-Grenadiers he had commanded a battalion in the Grenadiers, then the velites. Friederichs was serving with the Guard in Prussia and was sent back to Paris in March 1807 escorting flags and trophies taken at the bloody battle of Eylau in February 1807. His career followed a true Napoleonic trajectory; from humble soldier, he ended up being promoted to general of division in 1812, before dying from the after-effects of amputation after the battle of Leipzig in October 1813. The rest of the officers were arriving too, among them Pierre Delaitre, a man dubbed 'Pierre the Cruel' by his subordinates, and Captain Jacques-Marie Gillet, who had distinguished himself in Prussia in 1806; both were destined to meet terrible fates in Russia in 1812.

The conscripts selected to fill the eight active companies (four in each battalion, plus an additional depot company) came from the Class of 1807 and were soon submerged into a rigorous training programme overseen by their experienced NCOs. They were drawn from the empire's departments which included not only France but also Belgium, Luxembourg (then known as the Département des Fôrets), the former bishopric of Liège, parts of western Germany (Aachen, Trier and Cologne), as well as Savoy, Piedmont and Genoa.

The vast majority of the conscripts were 19 years of age and came from the burgeoning middle class and therefore were men of some education. Ambitious parents were keen to place their sons in a unit that could promise relatively speedy promotion, and present them with the possibility of having a son who was an officer after just a few years of service. There were some volunteers, also of good family, mingled in among the conscripts. Jean Michaud was one such. He belonged to the rural middle class, his relatively prosperous family living in Villognon in the

Charente. He arrived at the regiment on the 7th of February 1807 and was placed in the 1st Battalion. He found time to write to his parents two months later:

> I am writing to tell you that we will leave Courbevoie in eight days' time in order to join the army. That's why I asked you for some money. We are all uniformed, we all have the right equipment, and we are ready to leave. We have soup in the morning as well as meat, and there are potatoes in the evening. As far as pay is concerned, we have twelve sols per day, but they take back six of those for our rations, and then deduct a further three, and then reduce the rest still further.

These daily worries were soon overshadowed by orders for the regiment to set out for Germany. Napoleon had beaten the Prussians in 1806, but they continued to resist in the east and had persuaded the embittered Russians to renew the fight and bring their armies into Poland. The battle of Eylau, in February 1807, had been a draw in the Polish snows and now the emperor was calling on reinforcements to end the campaign with a bold stroke.

The 1807 Campaign

The Fusiliers-Grenadiers set out on the 20th of April 1807, being transported down the time-honoured road for French troops heading to Germany, passing through Metz and on to Mayence [Mainz]. Training continued en route with the conscripts being drilled into shape by the NCOs, who had been among the first to arrive at the depot (although Corporal Adrien-Jean-Baptiste Bourgogne, the famous memoirist, would only join the unit in July 1807). Sergeant Chrétien-Henri Scheltens, the earthy Flemish-speaking ex-sailor turned soldier, and originally from Brussels, was busy training the conscripts in their new duties: 'We drilled the troops throughout the journey,

5

every time we halted. Use of weapons was learnt as we marched along. There's no better training for the soldier than a campaign. He trains himself in order to take care of himself.'

Michaud and the others took time to get used to black bread and beer before they were swallowed up in the chaos of a campaign. Hard marching followed, and then came the unit's baptism of fire at Heilsberg, where it was thrown against a fortified Russian position in support of the struggling line infantry. The Russians withdrew in an orderly fashion that night, robbing the French of a clear victory. A few days later success was more certain when Napoleon caught the Russians poorly positioned on the wrong side of the river at Friedland. The French were triumphant, the Fusiliers-Grenadiers taking a lively part in the battle and then subsequently enjoying the fruits of victory in Berlin as the Russians and Prussians sued for peace. It was at this juncture that Corporal Bourgogne joined the unit. The blond NCO was aged twenty and stood 1.77 metres tall; he could read and write, had a good constitution and was good looking. He was placed in the 2nd Battalion and it is highly likely that he knew Scheltens.

Meanwhile, the festivities continued as the regiment was marched back through Germany and France (Scheltens says they were met with wine at every village along the way) to Paris to take part in parades marking the Peace of Tilsit, signed between Napoleon and Czar Alexander.

The Peninsular War

While the regiment was issued new clothes and equipment and sent out to enforced pasture in Normandy, a development that did not go down too well with the bored conscripts, Napoleon was just as restless. He set his sights on bringing the British to heel by closing the continent to British goods, and ruining her mercantile economy. The Russians had joined this great scheme (albeit reluctantly) and now the only loophole was Portugal, a loyal British ally. So it was that the French sent an expeditionary force down through Spain and into Lisbon. Not content with this, Napoleon began preparations to remove the Bourbons from the Spanish throne. His army was gradually fed into the country and began to occupy key positions. In February 1808 the Fusiliers were called out of their windy posting and sent south to the Spanish border. They were in Bayonne on the 30th of March 1808 and were soon established in the important fortress of Burgos, which dominated the road from Bayonne to Madrid. Napoleon felt in a position to act and had the Bourbons removed and bundled across the border into France. The Spanish people were outraged, and in May 1808 the inhabitants of Madrid rose in revolt (some of the Fusiliers-Grenadiers were present and were called in to suppress the fighting), soon followed by the rest of Spain. The revolt was supported by a British expeditionary force and fighting became general across the country. A French force was forced to capitulate at Bailen and the French evacuated Madrid. This brought an irritated emperor southwards, intent on restoring his power and prestige.

Napoleon hoped to win with conventional victories and led his army towards Madrid, sweeping aside opposition at Somosierra and entering the capital that December. The Fusiliers were prepared for a long campaign. Joseph Vachin, then a fourrier in the regiment's 2nd Battalion, wrote that: 'The people here are far less friendly. . . . all we have is bread, wine and meat, and without those things it would truly be the end of the world. Some say we will go to lay siege to Gibraltar, others that we will be sent to Cadiz to embark and be sent off who knows where.'

This did not come to pass, and instead the war changed in character. Spain's regular armies, outclassed and outfought, largely dissolved and the French were now faced by one of the most brutal guerrilla campaigns ever fought in Europe. There were countless atrocities; Scheltens remembered that they burnt down Medina del Rio Secco, put it to the sack and then torched it, just because someone had shot at Marshal Bessières.

The Fusiliers would remain in Spain for a year, largely serving in garrisons and in those isolated pockets of territory the French could hold on to, and picking up the regimental mascot, the dog called Mouton, near Burgos. If the fighting didn't kill or maim them, then disease often did. In September 1808 Vachin wrote a letter from Bayonne to his uncle, which throws some light on life in the Fusiliers in particular and a Napoleonic regiment in general:

> Here I am, I have finally got here, but not without suffering a great deal. It was only seven or eight days ago that the fever abated. I have had it since the 10th of July, and it affected me so much that I spent three days unconscious and five or six days in which, for hours at a time, I couldn't see. I am still very weak . . . but my appetite is returning and that is a good sign. You may be sure that my finances are in a perilous state after such a long illness. I would ask you to please be generous and to send me some money as soon as possible . . . I have never needed money as much as I do now for the staff at the various hospitals I have been in took advantage of my delirium to rob me of everything I owned.

Austrian Interlude
The Guard was recalled to Paris in February 1809. There was little time to reflect. Austria, which had been nursing a grievance since Austerlitz in 1805, and propped up with English gold, had launched an offensive into Germany and Napoleon was forced into waging war on two fronts.

Preparations for the war included the transfer of a number of individuals into newly formed regiments in the Young Guard, an increasingly common tendency with the Fusiliers supplying men to serve as sergeants and corporals to junior units such as the Tirailleurs-Grenadiers. It was not always an effective policy. As the Austrian war began, Captain Maurice Godet (born 1773), an officer in the Tirailleurs-Grenadiers, set out on campaign with a newly formed company in this unit:

> I left Paris at the head of my 260 men who had been granted the right to call themselves a company but were a company in name only. Imagine a collection of men drawn from eight different companies who barely had time to learn where they were, or were recruits, or worse, all commanded by an officer who was alone in knowing his duties, assisted by two second lieutenants who, before being nominated to the unit, had been velites, and four sergeants and eight corporals who were soldiers drawn from the Fusiliers-Grenadiers. It was with this raw material that I set out on the march, drilling as we went. In order to do the best that I could, I had the men practise marching in columns, deploy, and forming and dissolving platoons. All this every time we set out in the morning, every time we halted and every time we made camp. You can imagine the fatigue this induced, directing all these exercises and never letting them out of my sight. Whenever we halted at the end of the day's march, and as supper was being prepared, I had the soldiers taken to a field and drilled in the use of their weapons. Perhaps there my assistants might have been some use to me, but their contribution was far from helpful. They had never issued any instructions, and found that they needed to improvise. I had to be everywhere at once. Imagine, I even had to instruct the drummers in their business, even though I was a novice in the art but it was better than leaving them to their own devices . . . Finally, after spending twenty days on the march, and having repeated our drill time and time

again, we arrived at Strasbourg with my men at least resembling soldiers. But this style of life had worn me out, so much so that I fell ill shortly after our arrival.

Napoleon had the Fusiliers of his Guard rushed out from Paris, through Strasbourg to Bavaria, the Fusiliers forming a brigade in Curial's division. Vienna was occupied, and the French pursued the Austrian field army. They found it at Essling on the other side of the Danube. And it was here that the Fusiliers had one of their finest hours. The battle lasted two days, and the Fusiliers covered the retreat as the French fell back to the island of Lobau after an unsuccessful encounter with Austria's promising general, the Archduke Charles. Corporal Bourgogne was wounded, as were eight officers, and three officers (Piet, Duval and Caillat) were killed, along with a number of Fusiliers. The vagaries of life and death in a Napoleonic infantry regiment are perhaps best illustrated by the fact that the Fusilier Jean-Claude Comte was killed at Essling that May, but official notice of his death did not reach his family until the 25th of July 1810. Meanwhile, Duval was quickly replaced by Captain Félix Deblais from the Grenadiers, an amusing individual who has left a series of detailed and informative letters.

Promotions and rewards followed, perhaps to prop up morale after such a sanguine affair, and in early July 1809 a new colonel was appointed to replace Friederichs, who had been made a general of brigade. Just before the new colonel could take up his post, Napoleon gained his revenge on the Archduke Charles, beating him at the enormous battle of Wagram, a struggle which cost both sides thirty thousand men and brought peace a little closer.

The new colonel was Pierre Bodelin, born in 1764; by 1812 he was dubbed the oldest colonel in the army. He had fought in the royal army, joining up in 1782, but rose to become a lieutenant in the revolutionary armies by 1794. He was fortunate to have served under Napoleon in Italy and Egypt, and his steady rise under the empire saw him showered with awards and promotion. He ended up being nominated a general of brigade in 1813, and retiring due to ill health shortly afterwards (an incident that seems to have confused those tasked with inscribing the generals' names on the Arc de Triomphe, as his name is missing). Bodelin was strict, very much in the mould of the former colonel, and very close to another new arrival. The major commanding the 2nd Battalion had also been promoted, and Louis-Joseph Vionnet was brought in to replace him.

Vionnet had been born in the same year as Napoleon, but he was of more humble origins, as his father was an agricultural labourer and his mother made lace. He was born in Longeville, on the heights above the River Doubs near Switzerland, and his intelligence saved him from a career in the local iron mines and enabled him to become a teacher at the local school. The excitement of revolution carried him away from such scholarly pursuits and he volunteered, being elected an officer in the corps of local volunteers. He showed considerable aptitude as a soldier and as a survivor, avoiding the purges despite his Catholicism, and concentrating on fighting under the revolution's most famous commanders (Hoche and Bonaparte). He was in Italy from 1796 to 1800 and was a captain by the time the empire was established in 1804, going on to serve in the 12th Line at Austerlitz before being elevated to the Guard in 1806. Elevation to the Fusiliers-Grenadiers was a considerable coup for a man who had waited so long for promotion, but Vionnet was not grateful enough to be an out-and-out Bonapartist (in fact, in some parts of the Guard there was disdain for the soldier-turned-emperor), as events would show. He was, however, a professional officer, keen on discipline, strict, reasonably educated, with an interest in the world around him driven by a curiosity shaped by the Enlightenment.

The victory at Wagram gave the Guard some time to rest and recuperate, the Fusiliers-Grenadiers being billeted around Vienna and happily living off victuals supplied by the conquered Austrians. It was, by all accounts, a happy summer for the French. Then, on the 26th of October 1809, the Guard started to leave Vienna for Paris, the Young Guard leaving behind a number of exhausted men, or those too sick to follow. Back in the French capital the Fusiliers-Grenadiers were reformed; there was an influx of new officers and men drafted in from the Tirailleurs, while experienced NCOs and officers were sent out to bolster newer, and more junior, regiments. (This is what happened to Martin Bourgeois, born in 1779, who entered the regiment in March 1809 but transferred out to the Velites of Turin in April 1810.) On the 9th of October 1809 the prefect of the Indre and Loire wrote to the majors of the region stipulating that, after two years' service in the Young Guard, men who could read and write would be eligible to pass into the Fusiliers (although four volunteers from each department would also be admitted). The volunteers had to be 1.61 metres tall, know how to read and write, and be of 'a robust constitution, and capable enough, and intelligent enough, to become non-commissioned officers. A man who had served four years in the Fusiliers (including time in the Young Guard) would then be eligible to pass into the Grenadiers or Chasseurs of the Old Guard.' The Fusiliers-Grenadiers were still in Paris when the city marked the marriage of Napoleon to Marie-Louise of Austria, an act that was supposed to seal the peace between the continent's most recent rivals. Napoleon, accepted into one of the oldest ruling dynasties of Europe, was lavish to his Guard in the wake of this alliance. Bodelin was named a baron of the empire, Vionnet was made Chevalier de Maringoné. That summer the regiment was moved to Angers, the population of which was glad to see the soldiers' money, but resented the trials and tribulations of lodging so many demanding individuals in their homes. As an officer remarked, 'winter worries them, as they think about how much firewood they will have to burn'. Tension led to some scuffles, such as those which marked Napoleon's birthday on the 15th of August, an affair which saw townsmen and Fusiliers at odds, some fighting in the street, and the theft of Bodelin's epaulettes.

Back to Spain

The comparatively peaceful stay at Angers was welcome, but rudely shattered by news that the regiment was being sent back to Spain. Bodelin was surprised: two hundred of his men were on leave, and the rest in no particular mood to be sent to a war which continued to bleed men and money from the French empire, for precious little glory in return.

The mission the Fusiliers-Grenadiers would be required to perform was indeed far from glorious. The men were to be parcelled out into garrisons dotted along the vital lines of communications between Madrid and the French border. Those detachments not sent to sit out the campaign in Spanish castles were tasked with escorting convoys, protecting them from the roaming bands of cut-throat guerrillas, or organised into punitive columns sent out to chase and harry, or be chased and harried. It was hardly unsurprising, after a beautiful autumn spent along the Loire, that there were qualms. Not only because the contrast was so great, but because the war was far from popular, and far from being justifiable. The Spanish had, after all, risen up to defend their liberty.

Captain Godet of the 2nd Tirailleurs-Grenadiers was one of those also sent to Spain, and he described his thoughts and those of his fellow officers: 'Together we felt troubled that we were being obliged to go and fight in Spain and stifle an independence and sense of nationhood, something we ourselves had been fighting for against the northern powers. This repugnance was felt throughout our unit, but discipline pushed us on. We had to

13

go.' It would be an extremely tough campaign, Godet remembering that, 'I had believed that, upon entering the Guard, I would at least be granted a bit more rest, but I found myself obliged to carry out the hardest service I had ever endured.'

Scheltens agreed, noting that 'not a day passed by without us being shot at'. The danger was greatest when isolated or travelling alone. Captain Deblais of the regiment's 1st Battalion was initially dubious:

> They terrorise us by telling us a thousand frightening stories about this country, so that you think it should be covered in brigands and that you will be attacked every step of the way. So far [2nd of December 1810, on the way to Vitoria] we haven't seen any. In each of the little towns and villages along the way there are small garrisons of two or three hundred men, lodged and secured in some big house. They are there to ensure that the lines of communication remain open and escort the couriers by sending out fifty men to guard them. They are rarely attacked. These brigands are in reality bandits who prey on the main roads and only attack convoys or people too weak to resist. They never oppose troops who are well-armed and in good order, because there is nothing to steal. They go instead into the villages, force the people to feed them, and give them money. It is the scum of the country who support them, they have nothing to lose and act as spies.

The regiment passed through Bayonne, down to Tolosa and, by December 1810, was at Vitoria, with the troops lodged in the town's abandoned convents (billets that had not been abandoned by an army of lice, which led Scheltens to write that he was being eaten by vermin) and the officers billeted among the town's more wealthy inhabitants. In such places, and among such people, the French were relatively well received, and looked upon as providers of some security. The unit would stay there for six months.

Captain Deblais thought that the wealthy preferred the French: 'The rich who live in the towns and villages some distance from the main road, and where there are no garrisons, are pillaged and bothered by the brigands, and have been obliged to abandon their houses in order to seek protection with us. My host is just such a person, and they don't like the brigands at all.' He found life at Vitoria convivial: 'There is some society here, and it is quite nice and there is some amusement. We spend pleasant evenings at a house where I would like to be billeted. As the French have been here for three years, the place is a bit frenchified, and the women, it seems, are not savages.' The local men had 'formed a civic guard which patrolled alongside our own military'.

Corporal François Franconin of the Fusiliers-Grenadiers was perhaps even more pragmatic, and was of the opinion that 'The majority of Spaniards can't stand us, the rest tolerate us in order to ruin us by selling food to us at six times its real value.'

Scheltens, Deblais and others all remarked upon the dirty appearance, and dirty habits, of the Spanish. Scheltens found the lower class 'revolting' and commented that the 'peasants never wash their hands'.

Surgeon Lagneau, serving with a Young Guard unit, wrote a brief description of Logroño which included the telling remark that 'this town is quite dirty, they throw human waste out of their windows as used to be done at Marseilles'. Deblais contradicts him, thinking it 'a pretty little town with 7,000 inhabitants, in a charming location and in a delicious region'.

Outside the main towns, much of Spain was in ruins. Corporal François Franconin remarked that: 'It often happens that we shelter in houses that are half burnt down or demolished. All the houses in the villages and towns between

Vitoria and Madrid are like that. Burgos itself has been pillaged and sacked.' Franconin had been in the Fusiliers-Grenadiers until April 1810, when he was promoted to corporal and sent to join the Tirailleurs. It was perhaps a sign of the perceived superiority of the Fusiliers-Grenadiers that he yearned to be back with his old regiment, now (December 1810) newly arrived in the region. He wrote to his family with a request:

> It seems as though we will be here [Logroño] for some time. I do hope so. The food is good, the women are beautiful and the men are friendly. The regiment of Fusiliers-Grenadiers, which I served in, and which I really wish to serve in again, is at Vitoria, some forty-five miles away. If it would be possible to ask the general to write to Colonel Bodelin a second time, then perhaps my wishes would come true. If I should be lucky enough to go to Vitoria whilst they are still there, I would thank them for what they said to our good relative, namely to have me brought back into the regiment.

Napoleonic society was no different from any other, and connections were used to assist relatives in obtaining places within the unit. In 1812 Major Jacques-Marie Gillet's brother-in-law, Auguste Bernelle, was serving as a Fusilier in the regiment, with another brother-in-law, Jean-François, entering the unit as a second lieutenant in 1813.

Not that life in the unit was easy or overly privileged. The Fusiliers-Grenadiers had plenty of opportunity to feel sorry for themselves when they were sent out against the bands of Spanish guerrillas. There was some respect for these partisans, at least among the officers, but the lower ranks abhorred fighting such a dirty war. Franconin, for one, was not impressed:

> I didn't know what to think of those scoundrels before I had seen how brave they were – they aren't, and they only fight in the mountains when they are six times our number

. . . The brigands are not to be feared, however many of them there are; only their treachery is dangerous. I am as safe here as I would be in the middle of France.

Deblais thought that the guerrillas needed a superiority of three or four to one in order to fight and that, otherwise, they would just melt into the hills, necessitating an exhausting pursuit. The character of such punitive expeditions was harsh, and it wore out men, officers, uniforms, equipment and morale, as Deblais noted in January 1811: 'The day before yesterday, five hundred men from our two regiments came back. They had been out for two weeks. After having marched for two hundred and ten miles, and always through mountains or harsh terrain, they encountered two bands of these brigands, one mounted and the other on foot.'

The mounted troops belonged to Longa's band, whose 'troops are well-organised and he wages war skilfully'. In April 1811 Deblais and his company were sent out from Santo-Domingo (some forty miles from Vitoria) in pursuit of these men:

Our colonel received information that two hundred men, most made up of the famous Longa's cavalry, were at Belorado, a little town some twelve miles away. I was ordered to take a hundred picked Fusiliers from my company, and sixty mounted gendarmes. I was flattered to be given command of this little expedition. I set out at nine in the morning. The weather was not very good but three miles on we ran into their outpost of twenty men on horseback. I had them attacked by my vanguard and pursued them to within a mile of the town. My column followed on and I, with my scouts, led the way. We met a further twenty mounted brigands and firing broke out with my vanguard. I followed close behind to observe the enemy's movements. We eventually reached the town,

which is placed in a dip and, seeing that we were not
meeting much resistance, I had my cavalry charge in. The
brigands fled into the mountains, scattering to the left and
to the right. We pursued and then returned to the town,
where we were to spend the night. I returned victorious
with my two prisoners. I bought the horse of the
brigands' leader for 5 Louis. What will become of my two
prisoners? They say that I will have to have them shot.
But that's an act which is too inhuman and too barbarous.
I have treated them with kindness and do not regret it.

Hugo Longatin, of the Guard artillery, remembered that he only
took with him 'four pairs of trousers, three shirts, three pairs of
shoes, a tunic and a coat' when sent on these forced marches
against the guerrillas. Food was always a problem, with the
Fusiliers making soup out of the entrails of dead animals, and
Scheltens eating a mule for the first (and hopefully last) time in
his life. But this was still better than Bourgogne and Faloppa,
who tucked into beans accidently cooked in the fat of a hanged
man.

Frustration, combined with crude methods of waging total
war to suppress insurrection (skills honed during the
Revolution, and subsequently in Italy, Germany, Portugal and
Spain), led to atrocities and horror. Scheltens, as blunt as he was,
shied from some of the results:

I saw things in Spain which I simply dare not write down;
nobody would wish to believe they were true, despite them
being the truth. We rarely took prisoners. We were
commanded by General Roguet, who was as harsh with us
as he was with the Spanish . . . One day, as we traversed the
mountains of Old Castile, we arrived at a very pretty
village whose name I have forgotten . . . The Spanish had
established a piquet of twelve men, all lying around a large
fire. As we approached the sentry called out 'who goes

there?' Our officer replied, 'Spaniards, Regimento del Reyna.' At the same time he ordered us in with the bayonet. The Spanish tried to arm themselves but we were in amongst them, and the twelve men were massacred in less time than it takes to describe it. As this was going on, our men had surrounded the village, and then began to search the houses. We discovered some thirty-two officers who were en route to their regiments. Their uniforms were new and their escort consisted of just a few NCOs. Just one officer had managed to get away apparently. Just as well for him, as, on the following day, as we came back to the town we had left the day before, we saw General Roguet on a balcony, rubbing his hands together as he saw the fruits of our expedition. He ordered that eight officers should be shot at each of the town's four gates. Our detachment was lucky enough to be selected as executioners. In all my life I ever never seen anything as sad as this. These men pleaded with all the saints in heaven to be spared, the entire town was outraged. An hour later, it was all over. Such was the war in Spain!

Jacques-Joseph Boulanger, also of Roguet's division, remembered a similar massacre: 'We wage war on the brigands every day, and so it was that we took 1,500 of them. The general wanted us to shoot them, but the majority were killed with thrusts from bayonets.'

Scheltens remembered another such example when a Spanish cavalry officer was captured:

The French officer commanding us gave his prisoner, who could not walk very well, his horse, and the prisoner gave his word not to escape. As we entered our camp, General Roguet, already mounted and ready to leave, ordered our officer to draw up his report and to have the Spanish captain shot. He was taken into the courtyard of a burnt out convent, and they butchered the unfortunate man using bayonets.

Deblais also noted that: 'Formed troops always disperse the brigands, and they don't grant quarter when they get hold of any.' And he recalled that, when pursuing Mina's 'well-organised and veteran' men around Pamplona, his men, 'when they caught them, they shot them right away but they, less cruel, take prisoners'.

Scheltens blamed Roguet, a man nicknamed 'nada' by his men because he provided them with so little in the way of food. He was also a strict disciplinarian, shooting the cantinière's husband at Almeida in 1811 for stealing. Summary executions were common. As Scheltens said, 'Hardly a day went by without an execution or a hanging. The gallows at Burgos and Valladolid were always well encumbered.'

In addition to such treatment of hostages and prisoners, the troops turned to rewarding themselves with booty as villages were pillaged and then destroyed. Godet remembered that,

> At Molina d'Aragon General Roguet gave the command that everyone should set fire to their billets as they left. It has to be said that, of all the officers in the regiment, only Captain Galois, of the 4th Company, 2nd Battalion, a Parisian by origin, executed the order. The general did not punish those who refused the order, but Captain Galois was, for a number of days, the bête noire of our regiment. The soldiers had carried off anything they could get their hands on. A few had even demolished an organ in a church, got hold of some of the pipes and were now playing the kind of music that would have surely brought down the walls of Jericho.

Scheltens was also there, although he called the place Molinos, and he left the following account:

We entered the place in military fashion, and were given the order that, the following morning, as we heard the drums summoning us to assemble, we were to set fire to our billets and that the adjudants were to be held responsible for any houses that were not set on fire. In the house I entered, a father and his daughter had already been murdered, the unfortunate girl having been passed down through a number of hands before being killed. They had placed the father head first into a huge terracotta jar, and he had drowned in the oil. The next morning we set fire to our beds and we were barely outside before the flames were taller than the roof. All the houses had been set on fire.

Laying waste was accompanied by helping oneself to whatever could be saved, before or after the destructive fires. For the soldiers, it meant food and wine; for the officers, dismissive of such base instincts, it was often something more refined. Godet remembered that:

> At Medinaceli we occupied the palace of a duke. One day I saw Adjutant Ricardi turn up with a pile of French books under his arm. 'Where on earth did you find that lot?', I said. 'Good God, at the general's [Roguet's]. He is stripping his quarters of booty, and I got my hands on these.' I went over and found the general in the midst of the pillage and took what I wanted: a French-Spanish dictionary, Mariaha's ten-volume *History of Spain* and some poetry. The general reduced my loot by taking the dictionary off me.

Tirailleur Mignolet understood what effect such burnings, such devastation, would have: 'We are in a place where there are forty thousand guerrillas, and we encounter them every day, and things get worse and worse. A further four thousand have joined up this year, and we have burnt down towns and villages, which makes even more brigands.'

In the autumn of 1811 the Fusiliers were sent westwards from Valladolid and then Zamora in Spain towards Portugal, taking part in the offensive to prevent Wellington's British and Portuguese troops from pushing into Spain to support their Spanish allies. In March 1812 Roguet's division was based around Salamanca, preparing for a renewed offensive into Portugal. Mathieu Viatour, a Tirailleur, noted that,

> We have formed a corps around Salamanca with the intention of going into Portugal and we carried rations for twelve days but have lived off them for fourteen days. I still have some money. We were brought up into the line of battle, but the line infantry were sent in. We heard roundshot pass by. But the English pulled back and we had to let them go as we had no supplies.

Then came news that the unit was being withdrawn from the campaign, and was to march immediately for France. Roguet, in his memoir, noted: 'On the 2nd of March 1812 I took command of the 1st Brigade of Fusiliers . . . and set off for France. Each soldier carried 70 pounds of equipment, including food. We left Logroño on the 4th of March and arrived at Bayonne on the 10th.'

There was tremendous relief to be leaving Spain and all its woes. As they marched over the pontoon bridge that spanned the Bidassoa and marked the frontier between Spain and France, resplendent in newly issued grey-blue trousers, the Fusiliers-Grenadiers 'hurled their canteens, and cooking pots, into the river . . . all accompanied by tremendous cheers of "Long live France" and "Screw the Spanish". The soldiers telling themselves that there'll be no more bivouacs, we'll be billeted on the townsfolk.'

It had been an ordeal, perhaps best summed up by the taciturn Mathias Kayser: 'I was glad to get out, because things were very bad in Spain. You die there, they hang Frenchmen from trees.'

22

Russia in 1812

The Fusiliers were then transported through France in carts, coaches and (uncomfortable) wagons. Old Bodelin seems to have gone on ahead as he was in Paris on Saturday, 2nd of April. Roguet had received orders to hurry the troops along as the rest of the Guard had already left Paris: 'From there we were to follow the emperor's orders and travel post-haste to Paris. I arrived in Paris on 6th of April along with my division. It was quickly reorganised.'

Spain had necessitated great changes in the ranks, partly because of the wear and tear of warfare (the Fusiliers-Grenadiers did not lose any officers in Spain, but the Fusiliers-Chasseurs had one killed and two wounded in 1811), but also because the unit had been required to supply the Young Guard with replacements. The regiment had been kept up to strength not by volunteers (this was now frowned upon) but by the addition of literate conscripts drafted in from all the departments of a very much expanded French empire. For the first time there were Dutchmen, and there were Italians not only from Piedmont (such as Faloppa, Bourgogne's friend; Lagneau, future surgeon of the Fusiliers-Grenadiers, thought they were poor specimens as they suffered terribly from scabies) but also from Rome and Tuscany. NCOs had been transferred and despatched to depots and replaced by those from Young Guard regiments (the Fusiliers were now officially Middle Guard). Some officers left, including Deblais (to the Old Guard), Hennequin (to the Young) and Benoit Mayot, sent to the even younger Guard (the so-called Pupilles de la Garde), and so there were plenty of new faces. However, the regiment was at least full strength shortly after arriving in Paris, and was then thoroughly reviewed by Napoleon. It was being sent eastwards for the great confrontation with Russia.

France and Russia were nominally allies but many in Russia viewed that alliance as an imposition. Tensions over Poland and an economic policy that was detrimental to Russia's interests created a sense of mutual suspicion, and Napoleon, ever ambitious and seeking a quarrel which could restore a prestige dented by events in the Iberian peninsula, chose war over negotiation. By 1811 immense preparations were in hand, with a multinational army of half a million men forming up in Germany, including more reluctant contingents from Prussia and Austria. Napoleon hoped for a quick war, by force-marching his men into Lithuania to split the Russian armies, isolate them and defeat them in detail. It would be, he thought, the quintessential Napoleonic coup, and it would bring Russia to the peace table by the end of the summer.

History shows that this was not to be. But that May and June preparations were under way for the start of a great campaign under the eyes of a great leader. And the regiment was, by all accounts, at its greatest.

The Regiment

On the 4th of July 1812 the regiment had a complement of thirty officers, 1,391 men and twenty horses:

Colonel Pierre Bodelin
Captain adjudant major Julien Jean Joseph Rostein (known as Roustan)
Lieutenant adjudant major Pierre Delaître
2nd Lieutenant adjudant major François-Joseph Pasquy
Lieutenant Simon Boisseau
Surgeon Charlier
Assistant Surgeon Caïn
1st Battalion: Major Louis Joseph Vionnet
      Captain Louis Daix
      Lieutenant Gabillaud
1st Company: Captain André Gaspard Brousse (left the regiment before the campaign due to infirmity)
      Lieutenant Pernon

2nd Lieutenants Monnot and Jean-François Garbouleau
2nd Company: Captain Pierre-René François Goussin
 Lieutenant Philippe Joseph Crequy
 2nd Lieutenants Joseph Vachin and Tarrargere
3rd Company: Captain —
 Lieutenant Pierre Maupas
 2nd Lieutenant Pierret
 2nd Lieutenant —
4th Company: Captain Jean-Baptiste Desmoulins
 Lieutenant Louis Epailly
 2nd Lieutenant Rausy
 2nd Lieutenant Honoré Tamponet
2nd Battalion: Major Jacques-Marie Gillet
 Captain Adrien-Crépin-Marie Rouillard de Beauval
 Lieutenant Louis Egret
1st Company: Captain Jean Charles-Joseph Locqueneux
 Lieutenant Pierre Nicolas Guesdon
 2nd Lieutenant Rabourdin
 2nd Lieutenant Clement de Brerigel
2nd Company: Captain Saquoi
 Lieutenant Joseph Romain Colomb
 2nd Lieutenant Deville
 2nd Lieutenant Gauthier
3rd Company: Captain Ribet [?]
 Lieutenant Lyon
 2nd Lieutenant Henry Joseph Gustave Jean Grobert
 2nd Lieutenant Julien François Favin
4th Company: Captain Léonard Valentin Laborde
 Lieutenant Joseph Faucon
 2nd Lieutenant Jean-Théodore Serraris
 2nd Lieutenant Charles Laignoux

It seems that Captain Pierre François Maigrot commanded the regimental depot, along with Etienne Dingremont.

Sergeant Bourgogne, the famous memoirist, served in the same unit as Vionnet. He is shown here in 1831, wearing his newly awarded Legion of Honour. (Author's collection)

Vionnet himself, dressed in the resplendent uniform of a general in the Bourbon army. After the fall of Napoleon, Vionnet would act as a loyal supporter of the new Bourbon dynasty. (Author's collection)

This list includes some distinguished names and essential Napoleonic characters. Colonel Pierre Bodelin, commander of the regiment, was born in 1764 and fought in Italy and Egypt before the campaigns in central Europe in 1805, 1806 and 1807. He was promoted to command the Fusiliers-Grenadiers in July 1809, became a baron of the empire a year later and was promoted to general of brigade in 1813. He died in 1828. Then there was Major Jacques-Marie Gillet, born in 1777, who had spent much of his professional life in the Fusiliers-Grenadiers, being promoted to the rank of major in December 1811 and marrying the twenty-year-old Jeanne-Julie Bernelle, a protégée

Second Lieutenant Jean-Théodore Serraris, seen here in the uniform of an officer of the Kingdom of the Netherlands, survived the war and went on to become a general in Dutch service. He kept a brief but undeniably frank diary of his time in Russia.

General François Roguet commanded Vionnet's division in Russia, and had commanded the Fusiliers in Spain. He was strict, uncompromising and a very experienced soldier. The Fusiliers had already noted that he was as ruthless with the enemy as he was with his own subordinates. (Courtesy of Tony Broughton)

of the imperial family. He would be wounded in the legs at Krasnoe on the 16th of November, and would succumb to those wounds on the 8th of December.

The captains, too, were talented and experienced soldiers. First to be noted would be Captain adjudant major Julien Jean Joseph Rostein (known as Roustan or Roustam), given the role of enforcing orders and maintaining discipline. Born in the same year as Napoleon, he had also begun his career in the royal army, enlisting in 1786; surviving the tribulations of life in the infantry during the revolution, he emerged as a lieutenant in the Grenadiers of the Guard in 1807. He joined the Fusiliers in June 1809, just before Bodelin and Vionnet, and was promoted to Captain adjudant major in June 1811, while in Spain. He stayed with the unit until 1814, when he was transferred to the 12th Tirailleurs. He features quite heavily in Bourgogne's account, not surprisingly as he was the bridge between the regiment's senior officers and the regimental NCOs. He was the colleague of the far less amiable Pierre Delaître.

Captain Jean Charles-Joseph Locqueneux, born in 1774, was a volunteer of 1792. He joined the Fusiliers-Grenadiers in the summer of 1809, after service in the Grand Army in 1806 and 1807. He had been commended for bravery during the 1809 campaign, and entry to the regiment was the means by which he was rewarded. Following the Russian campaign, he would be assigned to command a battalion in the 4th Tirailleurs. Captain Jean-Baptiste Desmoulins was born in 1771 at Amiens and also fought in the Consular Guard at Marengo. He was in the Fusiliers-Grenadiers in 1807 and fought with them in Poland, Spain, Germany and Russia before transferring to the 10th Tirailleurs in 1813 and being wounded and captured at Leipzig. Captain Goussin had a similar record, but went on to serve at Waterloo (where he too was wounded). Captain Adrien-Crépin-Marie Rouillard de Beauval was younger, being born in Paris in 1779 to rather aristocratic parents. Joining the hussars in 1794, the young soldier proved his worth and by 1806 was a lieutenant in the 2nd Grenadiers of the Guard. He served in the Fusiliers-Grenadiers from 1811 and also left the regiment in 1813.

Such experience was also true of the more junior officers. Lieutenant Philippe Joseph Crequy was born at Fruges near Calais in 1769 and he too served in the Royal Army before the revolution and the Consular Guard when Napoleon took power, also serving at Marengo and, with the Imperial Guard, at Austerlitz, Jena and the Polish campaign of 1807. He became a 2nd lieutenant in the Fusiliers-Grenadiers in 1809, and lieutenant in 1811. He survived Russia and was promoted to major of the 82nd Line in 1813. Louis Epailly, born in 1774, had a very similar career path, fighting at Marengo and being promoted to a lieutenancy in 1811. He disappeared, presumed dead, in the closing days of the 1814 campaign. Pierre Nicolas Guesdon, born in 1777, had also fought in the Consular Guard as a grenadier and then as a sergeant. He was promoted to the Fusiliers-Grenadiers in 1807, being given the rank of 2nd lieutenant in the autumn of 1806. He was promoted to lieutenant in December 1811 after service in Spain but he would be less fortunate in Russia, dying during the retreat. Lieutenant Simon Boisseau, who had volunteered in 1793, served in the artillery and then transferred into the Guards in 1801, reaching the Fusiliers-Grenadiers in 1809.

The same pedigree applied to some of the more junior officers, although they were, on the whole, younger. For example, 2nd Lieutenant (adjudant major) François-Joseph Pasquy had been born in the Dordogne in September 1784, so can scarcely have remembered the revolution. But he served the empire faithfully enough and was awarded the Legion of Honour at Vilna in July 1812. The 2nd lieutenants Joseph Vachin, who could not face life as a shepherd in the wastelands above Montpellier and ran away to join the army, and Jean-François Garbouleau were also awarded the Legion of Honour at the same review, and Garbouleau was only twenty-five. Pasquy died in the summer of 1813, while Garboleau survived the wars, despite being hit by roundshot at Leipzig in 1813. More central to our story, 2nd Lieutenant Jean-Théodore Serraris emerges as a sardonic and resolutely professional soldier. Born in Kieldrecht, near Antwerp, in 1787, and thus only twenty-five when the Russian campaign began, he had volunteered to join the Velites of the Guard in 1806. Service in that particular finishing school saw him wounded a few months later at Jena in October 1806. He saw service in Poland in 1807 and was on guard duty when the emperor of Russia and Napoleon met to discuss peace on a raft in the middle of the River Niemen in June 1807. Alexander presented him with a purse of gold coins as a souvenir. In December 1811 he was transferred to the Fusiliers-Grenadiers and served in Russia, briefly returning to the Grenadiers of the Guard in early 1813 before being appointed as a major in the 11th Tirailleurs in April of that year. Following service around Antwerp in 1813 and 1814, he enrolled in the army of the Netherlands after the fall of Napoleon in 1814, rising up the ranks to that of colonel in 1833 and general in 1841.

We know a little, too, about the NCOs, thanks to the memoirs of Bourgogne and Scheltens. They were excellent material, honed by service in the field. After Russia, Bourgogne was promoted into the line, as was Sergeant Leboutte (145th Line), while Scheltens was raised to become a member of the Old Guard. Sergeant Major Pierre Richard Pierson, who had been with the corps since its foundation and was nominated to that rank at Smolensk in 1812, did even better, becoming a lieutenant in the Grenadiers in April 1813.

And the Fusiliers themselves? Perhaps they were some of France's best troops, again toughened, as Scheltens notes, by life on campaign:

> You had to have been through the wars of the empire to understand what a man can endure. Those long marches, lodged with the locals, and forced to communicate with them in their own language, or at least make yourself understood with sign language in order to get something to eat. We could tell the differences that existed amongst the peoples of the empire, the variety of manners, varied

A Fusilier-Grenadier and a Fusilier-Chasseur. The two regiments were brigaded together for most of their career.

religions, and the characteristics of peoples who lived between Madrid and Moscow. It is inconceivable that a soldier could survive the trials of those long marches, carrying a knapsack filled with equipment, with a bit of straw for bedding in the corner of some room, or, out under the stars, almost always without a fire, in the mud, exposed to torrential rain and forced to dry our clothes with nothing more than our own body heat.

The hardship would eventually take its toll, as Felix Deblais, now in the Old Guard, noted one day somewhere in the plains of Lithuania:

> I have passed the summer without eating a single piece of fruit, and without drinking anything but water. I am living badly. I have, for the last three months, being sleeping on straw and, for the most part, in the open air, exposed to all the whims of weather. That's military life on campaign. I feel that my health is no longer what it once was, it is fragile and I am often worn out. My body is full of aches and pains and I am nervous about winter. I don't know how I will be able to stand the onset of the cold, I fear the return of the rheumatism I had at Angers. I am not robust enough, we are but poor soldiers destined to die under the yoke or, after a thousand miseries, to retire with a modest pension and to nurse our infirmities. The emperor is big and fat.

Perhaps this attitude was true of Napoleon's army generally. The troops which had swarmed to the defence of the Revolution were long gone. There was still patriotism, but it expressed itself in the criticism of allies and in underestimating enemies. There was, as we see from Vionnet, an overabundance of officers' servants, and camp followers. To Russian observers, there was still, however, a certain Jacobinism when it came to the respect of discipline: 'The French sentries are badly turned out . . . and they don't keep in order when moving about, the men marching along as they please – some with their muskets on their shoulder, some at the waist with their hands thrust in their pockets. The French have dirty hands and none of them are clean.'

Another Russian observer noticed a certain frankness between officers and men: 'The tone used in their army is such that the common soldier is almost disrespectful towards a general and, if this individual is not his commanding officer, he

The glamour of war, with its resplendent uniforms, is given the lie by this sketch showing French troops cooking while on campaign. In 1807 the Fusiliers had worn out their uniforms and equipment in a single campaign, and by the time the regiment reached Moscow it may well have resembled these individuals. (Courtesy of the Anne S.K. Brown Collection)

can even criticise him to his face.' But in general it was a force led by a new aristocracy, one intent on keeping what it had acquired and one that, after 1812, would soon tire of war.

Vionnet's memoirs concentrate on the campaign in great depth, and this introduction will just sketch the outlines of the events as the Fusiliers-Grenadiers marched as part of the main body to Moscow and back.

The initial march through Germany was a delight, according to Scheltens:

> It was a veritable pleasure to march along such excellent roads, at the best time of year, and passing through such excellent countryside. We were billeted with the locals every evening, sometimes it was good, sometimes less so. We weren't always quartered amongst the rich, but the good Germans did what they could for us, even if they did so reluctantly. But the soldier never worries too much about the willingness of his host. When he is not given something, he takes.

An undated letter by Joseph Vachin echoed this optimism:

> Today I passed the Rhine for the seventh time, and I really do hope to cross it an eighth time. I am as well as might be expected of a man who has just travelled four hundred leagues without stopping, and we have another three hundred leagues to go before we reach the Niemen, travelling through the nicest country that can be imagined.

Then came Poland, and a dearth of food and fodder. The concentration of so many men in so small an area created a logistics nightmare. Horses began to die, and some artillery found it had to rely on oxen to get moving at all. Then, on the 24th of June 1812, three bridges were thrown across the River Niemen and the bulk of Napoleon's invasion force spilled on to Russian territory. Its flanks were covered by Austrians and

Saxons to the south, and Prussians to the north, and with comparative ease it pushed for Vilna, chief town of Lithuania. The Russians fell back, initially in some disorder, but soon with a discipline that astonished their foes. To keep up, or isolate the Russians from one another, the French were forced into a series of gruelling forced marches through the dusty summer days. Those days were tiring and long. Jean-François Chalsèche of the Fusiliers-Chasseurs noted on the 4th of August at Vitepsk (Vitsyebsk) that 'on Saint Jean's day there was no night, we had seventeen hours or more of daylight, but the day did not disappear'.

The toll was significant, not so much among the men of the Guard, but among some Allied units, and certainly among the horses. They fell like flies. Chalsèche's next comment was more prosaic: 'We have been marching for ten or twelve days now and it is hard to make our way through all the dead horses that have died on the road from fatigue and misery.'

The hard marching was accompanied by the usual problems of a campaign, magnified by the scale. At Vilna that July Marshal Mortier, commanding the Guard, noted that 'Lieutenant Garboulon [sic, he means Garbouleau] and 15 [later 17] Fusiliers-Grenadiers were to remain behind and act as the depot. Most of these men are afflicted by diarrhoea, dysentery or swollen legs.' The depot was housed in the university buildings.

Vilna was the first significant conquest, and the army received a ration of bread, pay and an imperial review at seven o'clock in the evening of the 8th of July. It was a review which saw a number of the Fusiliers-Grenadiers' officers awarded the Legion of Honour. From Vilna the offensive continued towards Smolensk, with Napoleon still hoping to ensnare at least one Russian army. He was disappointed, as he was in another hope. There was no general uprising, and the Lithuanians barely greeted the invaders, before, having been treated largely as an enemy population, they were constrained to supply large and regular amounts of food to make up for the supplies the Russians were burning as they fell back. Inevitably, the population was also dismayed by the plundering and marauding which followed in the wake of the army, most of it occurring away from imperial eyes. Napoleon did what he could to restrict too many outrages, shooting some looters in Vilna (and threatening anyone in his Guard caught committing disorders with instant transfer to the Line), deploying gendarmes to round up marauders and assigning his Guard to secure important towns. On the 17th of July Marshal Mortier wrote to Napoleon that:

> I have sent on ahead the 1st Battalion of the Fusiliers-Grenadiers to maintain order in Glubkoe and I have the satisfaction to report to Your Majesty that, up until the present, there have been no complaints. All the inhabitants remain in their homes and are well-disposed towards us. The region is attractive and well cultivated.

Smolensk was reached on the 16th of August after some stubborn rearguard actions. The Russians put up a spirited defence before firing the town and pulling back further into the interior. Napoleon, hesitating just slightly as to whether he should winter there, opted instead to push on the additional two hundred and fifty miles to Moscow, taking that risk in the hope that he could force the Russians to battle. The army badly needed rest, the seven-week campaign having reduced the forces available to Napoleon by half. The road to Poland was dotted with hospitals, and the decaying corpses of men and horses. The Fusiliers-Grenadiers were bearing up better than most. On the 23rd of August their strength was calculated at thirty-one officers and 1,296 men, ninety-five men fewer than on the opening days of the campaign.

The ordeal continued. At Gjatsk, on the 1st of September, Scheltens noted: 'The army was suffering a great deal. It arrived at Gjatsk. The rain had turned the roads into quagmires. Men and horses were dying in their thousands from fatigue and want. The bivouacs were cold and terrible.'

Three weeks after the fall of Smolensk, the Russians, now commanded by the wily Kutuzov, did turn to offer battle in defence of Moscow, forming up at Borodino. Napoleon, anxious not to let them get away, fixed them to the spot by a series of costly frontal assaults, while artillery on both sides wreaked unprecedented havoc. Spurning the chance to send his Guard forwards to deliver the coup de grace, and bereft of any characteristic brilliance, Napoleon watched as night fell on a field of horror. The Russians, bloodied but resolute, fell back, evacuated Moscow and drew the French still further in.

On paper Napoleon could have wintered in Moscow. There were supplies for the 100,000 men who had made it thus far but then, following orders from the city governor, the city was set alight. The army used the opportunity to thoroughly pillage what remained, despite the disapproval of men like Vionnet, and imperial orders only curbed the excess on the 20th or 21st of September. A disappointed Napoleon, who had expected to be met with an offer of peace, now faced a protracted stay in a city half-destroyed. Peace did not come. Czar Alexander, showing firm resolve, had decided not to negotiate, and had his generals apply pressure to the French flanks, menacing the long road back to Poland. Couriers were ambushed, convoys interrupted, and, for all the French pretence at normality, the weather got colder.

That pretence involved the re-opening of a theatre, and the digging of latrines by the walls of the Kremlin; an imperial order on the 23rd of September had fulminated that

> despite repeated warnings, the soldiers are continuing to relieve themselves in the courtyard, even under the windows of the Emperor himself; orders are now issued that each unit will set its punishment parties to dig latrines and, to avoid further complaints . . . buckets will be placed

in the corners of the barracks and these will be emptied twice a day, at five o'clock and at eight o'clock in the evening by men who are on punishment duty.

The Fusiliers-Grenadiers assisted in combing the city and the outlying countryside for supplies, while their colonel took part in the commission to try the incendiaries who had placed the French into such a predicament:

> The commission was formed of General Lauer, General Michel, General Saunier, Colonel Bodelin, Commandant Thery, Captain Jeannin and General Monthion. The commission met at the Dolgoroucky Palace in late September, passing judgement on the 24th of September 1812 on twenty-six incendiaries. It looked at the activities of a certain Smith (or Schmitt), an engineer who had established himself at the Voronzov Palace and set about designing a huge aerial balloon which would carry some infernal machine to destroy the French, all at the behest of the Russian government.

Of the twenty-six accused (one a portrait miniaturist, another the seventy-year-old servant of Prince Siberski), ten were found guilty and shot and sixteen were sent to prison.

The situation was untenable. The Russians were closing in, outmanoeuvring the Austrians to the south and gathering in resolute force to the south of Moscow. Preparations were finally made to quit the city. The Fusiliers-Grenadiers had received a detachment from the depot at Vilna and could boast a complement of thirty-two officers and 1,352 men (plus the dog, Mouton, now reunited with its parent unit) on the 19th of October 1812.

On that day Moscow was abandoned by the French, Napoleon leaving behind orders that the Kremlin should be blown up and, in a fit of pique, that the governor of Moscow's residence and that of Count Razumovsky should also be set

38

alight. Such actions did not bode well for the wounded the French had to leave behind them. The army set off, accompanied by a huge train of wagons filled with booty, or in the more prescient cases, loaded with supplies. The Fusiliers-Grenadiers had the unenviable task of escorting the painfully slow wagons of the imperial treasury.

The intention had been to push to the southwest, but a series of sharp actions persuaded the French to retreat back along the road they had come up in September. It wasn't long before they were recrossing the field of Borodino, which was, according to Scheltens: 'A mass of corpses half-devoured by animals and by carrion who took to the sky in dark clouds, darkening the earth and making sinister cries . . . it was a terrible scene.'

On the 5th of November, according to Scheltens, or the 6th (after a sharp frost the night before), according to Vionnet, it began to snow. Horses began to slip, or slowly starve, and wagons and artillery encumbered the retreat. The men, too, went hungry. Cossacks, shadowing to the left and to the right, prevented the search for food, and the French began to drop. All eyes were on Smolensk and the warehouses General Charpentier and his assistant Jomini had supposedly filled with supplies. The army broke in on the 9th and sacked the city comprehensively. The Fusiliers got some flour, but little rest. On the 14th the retreat continued but the entire army was placed in grave danger when the Russians swung across the road and separated Napoleon and his vanguard from the corps dragging along behind. Here the Russians were checked at the bloody battle of Krasnoe, but at considerable cost. The Fusiliers-Grenadiers suffered heavily but the road was again open and the retreat continued. It was around now that Sergeant Bourgogne became separated from the unit, only rejoining it a week later:

> A moment later the Fusiliers-Chasseurs appeared, our regiment was brigaded with them. They were much reduced in number. Our regiment was separated from

them by some artillery the horses of which had difficulty keeping going. A moment later I saw the regiment marching in two ranks on either side of the road, catching up with the Fusiliers-Chasseurs. Adjudant-Major Roustan was the first to see me and he called out 'Ah, poor Bourgogne, is it really you? They said you had died in the rear and here you are alive and in front of us! So much the better! Have you seen any men of the regiment in the rear?' I replied that for the last three days I and one other had been in the woods in an attempt to escape from the Russians. Mr Serraris told the colonel that, since the 22nd, I had been left in the rear, being ill, and that just one thing surprised him and that was to see me again. Then my company arrived and I took up my post on the right without my friends realising. When they noticed, they surrounded me and asked me lots of questions which I could barely answer, so overcome was I by the reunion and feeling that I was now amongst my family. I looked at my company and saw that it was much reduced. The captain [Laborde] was missing, all his toes had fallen off and nobody knew quite where he and the poor horse he had been given to ride had got to.

Events now took a turn for the worse. The Russian armies from the south, having slipped past the Austrians and seized Minsk, had reached the River Beresina. Other Russian divisions, swinging down from the north, were applying pressure to the French right flank. The one good bridge over the Beresina, at Borisov, had been burnt and the French, with courage born of despair, threw two temporary bridges over the river and struggled across, forcing a passage through to Vilna. It was a terrible episode. Scheltens gave a terse description:

A confused mass of women, children, men and horses, all dying of hunger and cold, surged forward as one to cross the bridges, all under the fire of the Russian artillery. A few fugitives threw themselves into the water, others were pushed in. They struggled to cross the river by swimming, or grabbing onto the ice, and passing from one block to the other.

The bridges were set on fire after all efforts to get the stragglers across expired. Thousands were left stranded, mostly to perish from want or disease, and the survivors made for Vilna. The army was now starving: Scheltens ate a dog, Bourgogne ate a blackbird. Napoleon abandoned the army at Smorgoni, heading back to Paris to raise a new army and impose his will on an empire troubled by doubt and rumour.

The army that was left behind in the snow struggled into Vilna that December. Scheltens was still with the Fusiliers-Grenadiers, noting that 'there were some thirty of us, all told, though not including the officers. We pillaged the imperial staff's stores. We found some good flour there, some lard, good oil, rice and fine wine, even some Champagne and some brandy. We spent the night cooking pancakes, or baking bread.'

At Vilna Scheltens saw another of our eyewitnesses kill a man while looting the warehouses:

Our lieutenant Serraris was coming out of the palace where we were quartered. He had a ham under each arm. A soldier attempted to block his way, and grab one of the hams. By way of response, he got hit on the head by one of the hams, with such force that it knocked him down. It is only fair to add that the man was so weak that it did not take much to kill him.

The Fusiliers loaded what they could on four small ponies, and quit a Vilna menaced by the arrival of the Russians. They left their surgeons behind, tending the thousands of sick and wounded. Just outside the city, on the slopes of Ponari, they came across hundreds of abandoned vehicles, including a sledge.

41

Scheltens passed one containing an officer whose driver had made off with the sledge's horse: 'Wrapped in a huge cloak, but with frozen feet and hands, he begged me to kill him because he knew that he could not survive for long in such a situation. I had loaded my musket to carry out this deed, but I reflected that he would probably die without my involvement. I left him, but I could hear his entreaties for some time afterwards.'

Among the vehicles abandoned on the ice were the imperial treasury wagons, their draught animals unable to pull them up the hill. Scheltens nearly took a sack of 50,000 Francs but found it too heavy, preferring to stuff some gold coins into his trousers and then transferring them to a fur bonnet he kept hanging around his neck.

A few days later the army limped over the bridge at Kovno and back into Poland. Colonel Bodelin watched the sad remnants of the regiment march out of Russian territory, saying to them,

> Come on, my children! I won't tell you to have courage, as I know you have that already for, during the three years we have been together, you have given ample testimony to that on every occasion, and especially so during this terrible campaign, and in every battle that you have been involved in, and in the endurance of every privation. But remember this – just as there are risks and dangers which have to be endured, so there is also glory and honour, and there are rewards too for those who by constancy and determination emerge with honour.

The survivors headed for Königsberg, halting at Wirballen and Intersburg, where the remnants were reorganised. The Fusiliers-Grenadiers were shattered. They counted two hundred men in the ranks. Major Gillet, Captain Delaître, and Lieutenants Guesdon, Pierret and Rausy had died during the retreat (the latter at Kovno, at the end of the ordeal); Major

Vionnet and Captain Ribet had been wounded. Surgeon Charlier had been left behind at Vilna and taken prisoner as, in all probability, had his assistant Caïn ('an intelligent young man, full of zeal', according to Baron Larrey). Pierre Schan, a 21-year-old Fusilier, had fallen into enemy hands at Orsha, never to be seen again. Jean Balazot was luckier: he was captured by the Russians at Orsha but returned from captivity in 1814. Some stragglers caught up, but the vast majority of the regiment was left in the Russian snow.

Germany and France

An attempt was made to rebuild the regiment. Officers and cadres scurried back to Paris, to be reviewed by a shaken emperor on the 16th of March 1813. A former Fusilier, Frix Dupouy, who was transferred to the Tirailleurs and was one of the few wounded at the Beresina to make it back to France, appeared on crutches before the emperor at Trianon:

> He fixed me with his penetrating gaze, he asked me the following question: 'You have been wounded?' The question surprised me as it was uttered by a man who had, a thousand times before, revealed his ability to read men, even if they had something to hide. 'I asked if you have been wounded,' repeated the emperor. 'Yes, sire,' I replied. 'Where?' 'At the passage of the Beresina.' 'Despite all that,' he added, 'the climate did not devour you. Are you recovered?' 'Not yet, sire.' 'You will be soon. I'll make you a second lieutenant.'

Following this review, many of the officers were promoted. Bodelin was made a general, despite his exhaustion. Serraris was transferred to the 11th Tirailleurs of the Guard, while Vionnet was promoted to colonel and to the command of the 2nd Tirailleurs. Joseph Vachin went into the Line to serve as a captain. Of the officers, only Rostein, Pasquy, Laborde,

Colomb and Lyon remained with the Fusiliers; the rest were moved on.

Among the NCOs, 1813 saw the start of a similar process. Sergeant Bourgogne was also made an officer in the Line, becoming a second lieutenant in the newly raised 145th Regiment, along with his comrade Sergeant Leboutte. Scheltens passed into the Grenadiers of the Guard, as did Sergeant Pierson. Sergeant-Major Nicolas Oudiette was a rare case; he remained with the Fusiliers, being promoted to second lieutenant.

The rank and file, however, had to be almost entirely replaced. So it was that Surgeon Lagneau arrived to serve in a very different regiment of Fusiliers-Grenadiers, one almost entirely reconstituted from conscripts: 'The men destined to fill up the ranks are already gathering at the barracks at Courbevoie. The organisation will take some time because they have sent us a large number of conscripts from the classes that have not previously been called up. There is much to do.'

This regiment was being prepared for a war that would see Napoleon forced to face not only the threat of vengeful Russians pouring into Poland and eastern Germany, but also a Prussia that had decided to switch sides and once again fight the French. The Fusiliers-Grenadiers went off to fight in the spring of 1813 campaign in Saxony, being blooded at Lützen, where the young regiment was badly mauled by Russian artillery, according to Fusilier Dufraisne: 'I was horrified by the sight of a roundshot that killed Marshal Mortier's horse, carried off two legs in the 2nd Company, the arm of our lieutenant (who died) and ended up killing a comrade right next to me.'

The Fusiliers then acquitted themselves well at Bautzen and, after the armistice that punctuated the war, and brought the Austrians in on the side of the Russians and Prussians, at Dresden. All was swept away that autumn at Leipzig, and, following that monumental defeat, the French were ejected from

Germany and Napoleon found himself isolated and obliged to defend French soil. This he did with consummate skill, the Fusiliers-Grenadiers sharing in the glory, but suffering heavily at Montmirail, La Fère-Champenoise (where Lagneau was wounded) and at the final battle at the gates of Paris. Napoleon's abdication and the return of royal rule saw the disbandment of the unit, with the personnel supposedly being transferred into the Royal Grenadiers, then forming at Metz; in fact, many simply went home (and were regarded as deserters by the restored Bourbon government). The Hundred Days saw many re-enlist, fighting as part of the Grenadiers at Waterloo, but the Fusiliers-Grenadiers would never be reformed. It was the end of a short, but distinguished, career.

But what of Major Vionnet, Baron Maringoné since the 14th of September 1813? He, like many others, welcomed the return of the Bourbons, his conservative tendencies leading him over to Calais at the end of April 1814 to greet the returning Louis XVIII. He was tasked with forming the newly created 8th Line but then a period of inactivity followed, during which he was made a knight in the Order of St Louis, and married the 25-year-old Barbe Beuzelin at Ternes, the couple preferring to live in their flat in the Rue Richelieu in Paris. The return of Napoleon during the Hundred Days was an unwelcome shock, but Vionnet refused to support the emperor and, when it was all over, he emerged sporting a white cockade and loudly demonstrating his loyalty to the Whites. He went out to escort the king back to Paris (travelling in Sir Sidney Smith's carriage), siding resolutely with the royalists more vengefully than ever before. IIe was again promoted and given command of the Rhône department. There he achieved notoriety for his persecution of Bonapartists, particularly in Lyon, where events led to the execution of General Mouton-Duvernet, a loyal supporter of the emperor who had been in hiding in the city since Waterloo, and became immersed in intrigue which, ultimately, reflected badly on him. He was forced to resign, and spent the intervening years writing his memoirs until, in 1820, returning to the ranks and being made a viscount. Strangely, he now found himself once more sent off to Spain, commanding a brigade in the armies sent by France to assist the Bourbons in suppressing the liberals there in 1823. He finally retired from the army in 1831 and died in 1834.

The Memoirs

The Advance to Vilna

On the 23rd of June 1812 we arrived on the banks of the River Niemen. The weather was rather warm but very fine. The French army was full of enthusiasm and confident in the abilities of its leader. It was a superb and well trained force.

Indeed, I had never embarked upon a campaign under more encouraging auspices. I commanded one of the most beautiful and bravest battalions of the Guard (the 1st Battalion of the Fusilier-Grenadier Regiment).[1] I was keen to start and confident about what was to follow. I had a number of servants and three wagons loaded with supplies and provisions in the convoy following along in the baggage train in the wake of the army.[2]

On the 24th we started to cross the Niemen by means of three bridges which had been put up the night before.[3] Just then the weather took a turn for the worse and a terrible storm began. It killed or wounded a number of men and horses. We were particularly worried that the thousands of caissons in the artillery park might be hit by lightning.

We perhaps should have seen this storm as a fatal omen – the Romans, more superstitious than ourselves, would not have gone a step further.

On the 27th, after brushing aside some light resistance, we entered Vilna [Vilnius]. The population met us with considerable enthusiasm. We were lodged amongst the inhabitants and they welcomed us with charming hospitality, something which made our stay most agreeable.[4]

On the 10th of July we continued the advance.[5] On the 11th we were billeted at Lavarischki. On the 12th we reached Mikailchki. On the 13th we were at Cheki, and at Danielowicz on the 14th. On the 15th we reached Glubkoe. We had been passing through a region which was generally beautiful and well cultivated. But most of the villages had been devastated by our vanguard and this perhaps sowed doubt in the minds of those very same Lithuanians we had come to liberate.[6]

Glubkoe is a small town with rather a depressing air. It is almost entirely populated by Jews.[7] We stayed there for two days, after which we received the order to pursue the Russian army in the direction of Vitepsk. We stayed drawn up at Sienno whilst the cavalry under the King of Naples[8] and the IV Corps took part in the victories at Ostrovno and at Vitepsk.

On the 28th of July we entered Vitepsk and spent some time there whilst the rest of the army caught up. The truth was that

A sketch by Albrecht Adam, who was attached to Eugene's IV Corps, showing French and Italian troops on the march in Russia. Note the emaciated horses. The scythes were important as the French tried to live off the land. (Author's collection)

A second sketch made that summer shows men and animals in a state of complete exhaustion, advancing through territory already stripped bare by the retreating enemy. (Author's collection)

ever since we had crossed the Niemen the army had suffered quite terribly. Not because of enemy action but because there was an absolute shortage of provisions and a complete lack of administration.[9] The country through which we were marching had already been stripped by the Russians who, having been beaten, were falling back in perfect order whilst we, the victors, came on in complete disorder. This was something which would have disastrous consequences should we suffer a setback.[10]

We stayed at Vitepsk until the 10th of August.[11] The emperor reviewed us a number of times and busied himself in dealing with the administration, matters concerning food and the hospitals.[12]

Sometimes the advancing troops would strike lucky, as with this marauder pictured in early August 1812. (Courtesy of the Anne S.K. Brown Collection)

The Battle for Smolensk

On the 10th of August we marched off for Smolensk carrying with us a fortnight's worth of rations. We marched along the great road which ran from Orsha to Smolensk, crossing over the River Rasana by means of a pontoon bridge.

On the 16th we came within sight of Smolensk. We had thought that the Russians would withdraw after having evacuated the town but this was not the case. They had in fact fortified the city. The emperor drew his army up in the form of a semi-circle, with each flank resting on the Dnieper. On the 17th an assault was launched against the city. A heavy bombardment proved insufficient to breach the thick walls which encircled the city. The Russians killed or wounded some 5,000 of our men.

50

On the morning of the 18th we were informed that the Russians had quit the city after having set fire to it. They had crossed the Dnieper. A great deal of firing broke out along both banks of the river and this continued for much of the day. That evening we entered Smolensk and, on the 19th, we learnt that we had won a victory at Valutina.[13]

Smolensk was the first serious battle of the campaign. This illustration shows French troops watching as an assault is launched against the town. (*Author's collection*)

On the 20th of August the emperor inspected the battlefield at Smolensk and I was part of his escort.[14] He then assembled a council of war involving the marshals and the generals of division. He raised the issue of whether to halt here or to march forwards and onwards to Moscow. Everyone, with the exception of Davout, who wanted to be King of Poland, had wisely

51

The fighting ruined Smolensk, and the miserable inhabitants fled into the outlying countryside. (Author's collection)

counselled that we stay in Lithuania.[15] Nevertheless the order was then issued for us to advance.

At eight o'clock on the morning of the 24th of August we were under arms and ready to begin moving forwards. We were kept waiting for ten hours in this position. Finally, at around seven o'clock in the evening we set off and marched for the whole night. At eight o'clock on the morning of the 25th we paused for a short moment of rest at Panovo and then crossed over the Borysthenes[16] at Solovie and camped around four miles further forwards of that place. We were placed in closed columns on either side of the road. The heat was excessive and the exceptionally fine dust made breathing extremely difficult and it really stung the eyes. I fashioned some spectacles from some green glass and these proved to be very useful.

On the 26th of August we camped in the middle of some

hemp fields, close by Osviate and with a small tributary running in to the Borysthenes to our right. The night of the 25th to 26th had been very cold, but the day itself was splendid.

On the 27th of August we passed through Dorogobutz and camped by a monastery around nine miles further forwards, this time in a field of rye.

It rained a little on the 28th. We camped in a wood close by a little river. On the 29th of August we reached Vyazma, a large and pleasant city situated at the source of the River Oka which is a tributary which flows into the Volga at Novgorod. The Russians had set fire to their stores but the fire had spread to the town itself and much of it had been consumed by the flames. The same had been true of the entire country between Smolensk and Vyazma. The Russian rearguard set fire to something and the negligence of the French troops, who got inside the houses to find food, meant that the fire spread and destroyed everything else. The picture presented by such a conflagration was indeed hideous to behold. One could see up to ten villages burning at the same time. Between the 25th and the 29th of August it was so hot that if a fire was lit on the ground it quickly spread and this meant that entire forests were quickly reduced to smoking ash. The inhabitants, terrified at the prospect of an approaching enemy, would abandon their homes and goods and would retreat along with the Russian army. Hardly anyone was left behind. The elderly, children, everyone fled at our approach.

Vyazma is around 110 miles from Smolensk and 190 from Moscow. It is situated in a pleasant position at the heart of a very fertile region. I counted around forty bell towers or domes in the area. The rain that fell during the night of the 28th to 29th August abated the fires in the villages a little and the prospects for saving the rest of this unfortunate region began to feel more likely.

On the 30th of August we rested and had an inspection.

On the 31st we occupied a camp which had belonged to the

Russians close to a place called Teplucha. There was such a shortage of water that it was almost impossible to get hold of any to make some broth or soup, or to have any to drink. We only generally washed our hands or our faces when we found a river. Sentries had to be posted at wells to ensure that the soldiers would not squabble over some water which was often stagnant or brackish.

On the 1st of September we marched on to Tzarevozalo-michlchte, passing along a very bad road until we made camp. There was a terrible storm that night with thunder and lightning. The lightning struck at a number of points in our camp and one of the soldiers was killed and quite a few were wounded. The Russian army had burnt down the bridge as it was leaving, as well as some of the town. We spent some time trying to repair the bridge. This town is 170 versts[17] from Moscow.

On the 2nd of September we should have remained in our camp but the officer who was supposed to bring this order to us only reached us as we neared the town of Gjatsk. We took up quarters in the suburbs and along the main road. The only inhabitant to remain in the town was an old woman and she simply did not want to speak to us.

Gjatsk is large and pretty and the principal town in the district. Some of the houses boast a very elegant architecture on the outside and are very spacious on the inside. The streets are wide and straight, but they are badly paved. Whenever I had a few moments to myself, I would go out and about visiting the churches. I was particularly taken with the one which is to be found just outside the town on the Moscow road. It is built in the shape of a Greek cross, with a tower at one end and a dome above the choir at the other. The church was divided into three parts: the entrance, the nave and the sanctuary. The altar is to be found in the sanctuary and it consists of a relatively simple square table. The sanctuary is divided from the nave by three doors which bear upon them carvings portraying scenes from the Old and New Testaments. The walls are covered in paintings on wood displaying holy images. The background on almost all of these paintings is made from gold leaf, the colours are very rich and the faces are very well depicted. However, the fact that all these figures have the same pose renders them rather monotonous. One other fault is that the body is not usually in proportion and so they seem relatively bigger than they should really be. I noted the study of a head of an old man which could have been carried out by a master.

In the church's sanctuary there was, just above the door, a painting of the Last Supper which seems to resemble that by Leonardo da Vinci. In Russia it is very common to see a great number of little paintings on wood which show the entire life of someone or a story – for example, John the Baptist's life, the story of the adulterous woman, Saint Peter's life.

The Russians have generally adhered to the Greek style for their churches and, in truth, the amount of ornamentation is prodigious. It must be said that their opulence and freshness puts the miserliness of our own churches to shame. The religious books and everything that is used during mass are of such an elegance and magnificence that must be seen to be appreciated. I noted especially an ingenious way of representing the holy trinity on a thin painted tablet. This painting had the Holy Father on one side and Jesus Christ on the other with, in the centre a screen composed of thin strips of wood with an image of the Holy Spirit represented as a kind of dove. It was done in such a way that the figure of the Holy Father was on the right, that of the Son was on the left and that of the Holy Spirit could be seen in the centre. All three could be seen separately but never all together. This icon was designed to show the Russian peasants that the Father, the Son and the Holy Ghost formed but one god, just as they formed just one painting.

That same day, the 2nd of September, the emperor had the

generals of division send in a precise roll call of the exact number of combatants present in the ranks of each unit and of the number of cartridges available to each man. On the 3rd the same process was repeated by the generals of brigade and after this orders went out that we should now prepare for battle.

Borodino

On the 4th of September we set out at around six o'clock in the morning marching in column by platoons or sections. Sometimes we covered the flanks but, on the whole, there was much disorder. We were obliged to halt for quite some time whilst the I and III Corps, which had been in the rear, were allowed to pass. Then we advanced in columns with artillery and cavalry in the centre. We made camp close by Drovnino on the shore of a lake and some little distance from a small wood. The Russian army had occupied that position the day before. At five o'clock the following morning there was a sharp frost.

At half past nine on the 5th of September the army marched forwards. The weather was fine, although at around ten o'clock a cold wind began to blow and this lasted for much of the rest of the day. We passed close by Gridnevo, a small village where there is a monastery for Orthodox monks belonging to the Order of Saint Basil. In Russia, there are a great number of religious houses but they all belong to just one order – that of Saint Basil.

The monastery at Gridnevo is really quite large and is surrounded by magnificent gardens enclosed within walls. The entrance gate is opposite the church and it has above it a bell mounted within a miniature triumphal arch. The church has a dome which has four bells mounted on obelisks at each corner. The monastery is detached from the church and is set some way off on a small hill which allows it to look over the surrounding area. The monks and the entire population had abandoned their homes. The Russian army had set fire to two bridges and this fire had spread to the village which, as a result, had been almost totally destroyed. The fact that the wind was now blowing in the opposite direction led us to hope that the monastery itself would be spared by the flames, as well as some of the surrounding buildings. The region around here is well off and the soil fertile, producing all kinds of grains.

We arrived at a river and drew up facing the Russians. At around a quarter past five that afternoon the firing began on both flanks of our position; it was heavy and it continued until nightfall. For much of the time it was heavy. The enemy was pushed back and our army camped on the field of battle. The Guard made camp close to a village and with a ravine and stream before it. It was drawn up in three lines and kept sufficient distance between them so that we could form squares should the need arise. The night was very dark and there was some rain.

It continued to rain on the morning of the 6th of September. At seven o'clock we heard the cannon open fire and an attack was launched against the point where the two small streams enter the River Kaluga. The terrain, which at first sight might seem to be rather flat, is in fact undulating and dissected by a number of ravines. The banks of the river are steep-sided and difficult to cross.

The Russians had constructed a number of batteries, which led us to believe that they had been planning to defend this position but our rapid advance had meant that they were unable to finish the works. Now, just before our attack on the 6th was about to begin, they were in the following position: their right rested on a small stream which was a tributary of the Kaluga; their centre was positioned around Borodino; and their left rested on a small hill which was covered in trees and which was now protected by redoubts. Beyond this hill one could make out a redoubt on some heights with some accessible ground before it. Their line was protected by the two streams and they were in a sort of semi-circle. It stretched over some distance but it was easily visible. The attack began on the Russian right close by a mill – the ground that stretched to the River Moskowa was protected by a few Cossacks, who spent the entire day resting just beyond the range of the guns.

No sooner had the action begun on our left than we also launched an attack on our right flank on the woods dominating the Russian left. It was relatively easy to determine that this was the weak point in their position and that Napoleon would seek to break through here by means of a vigorous attack. The attack succeeded, despite a most stubborn resistance, and the Russians tried a number of times to retake the position but were, again and again, beaten off. The voltigeurs advanced against the redoubt, which was about the range of a cannon from the woods. They were beaten back a number of times but, when supported by a column of infantry and by cavalry advancing and turning the position, the redoubt was carried by assault. A great deal of skirmishing continued but, as the night was dark, both sides soon preferred to pull back and husband those forces available to them for the next day.

The night was wet and cold. The Guard was placed in three lines, with its right resting on the position occupied by the Russians between the two streams. General Kutuzov,[18] by selecting this position, had anticipated the emperor's favourite tactic of attacking the enemy in the centre, splitting it in two and paralysing both flanks by means of preventing them from communicating with each other. If he had made use of this tactic here, our troops would have been exposed to fire from both flanks and our centre might then in turn have been broken. But the emperor was not to be fooled. After carefully studying the Russian position he drew up a plan which, I believe, would consist of us breaking the enemy's left flank, and acting so as to cut the enemy's line of retreat towards Kaluga and throw them back towards Moscow.

If General Kutuzov had managed to delay the engagement for a number of days it is highly likely that he would have defeated us without even bringing us to battle. The truth was that an enemy more powerful than all the armies in the world was besieging us in our camp. That enemy was famine and it was carrying off more men than cannon fire. Our soldiers were finding it very hard to even stand on their feet; many of them were falling down on the roadsides and were unable to continue. And it was there that they died, uncared for and cursing the commander who was sacrificing them for his boundless ambition.

The night of the 6th to the 7th of September was terrible. We spent it camped in the mud, without campfires, surrounded by the dead and the wounded, whose pitiful cries and gestures broke our hearts. The Russians were camped opposite us, forming a kind of amphitheatre. The sight of their camp fires made for a unique spectacle and contrasted sharply with our own situation. We were actually shifted from one position to another and it was only around midnight that we finally established ourselves in one place.

On the 7th of September the battle of Borodino began. The fighting started at around five o'clock in the morning. The Russians had their right flank resting on the point where the Kaluga joined the Moskowa river. It was a position strengthened by three redoubts which cut the road to Mojaisk [Mozhaysk]. The Russians were positioned along the river as far as the deep ravine at Borodino village. Their position was thus protected by the natural features of the terrain: by the river and by some heights. This was augmented by the three redoubts, two of which were replete with twenty pieces of artillery in each one. To the south was the Great Redoubt, which formed the very centre of the Russian position. Behind this was a shallow valley in which were massed large bodies of enemy infantry. The left of the Russians was placed by some woods and their entire flank was protected by six redoubts placed before their position. Behind these were more woods. To the right and left of these, the Russian army was drawn up on some heights with the Great Redoubt forming the hinge at the position's right angle. This formation had the advantage of centralising the forces available to the Russians whilst forcing ours to act over a more dispersed area.

Just when the battle was about to commence, the following order of the day was read out to all the units:

> Soldiers, here is the battle you have longed for. Victory now depends on you; it is essential to us, it will bring us everything we need, good winter quarters and a quick return home. Conduct yourselves as you did at Austerlitz, Friedland, Vitepsk and Smolensk, and may posterity ever more cite your conduct on this great day; may they say of us: 'They were at that great battle beneath the walls of Moscow.' From the camp at Mojaisk, the 7th of September 1812.

At a number of points along the line this order was read out whilst the guns were already firing. It provoked considerable enthusiasm and was the signal for the launch of the main assault. There never was a bombardment like it, neither in terms of its intensity nor in the period it lasted. It was so loud that one could not distinguish the noise of a particular cannon. It was just a continuous rumble which shook the very earth. Towards nine o'clock the number of wounded was already considerable. We could only imagine what the result of all this might be, given that this was just the beginning of a long day. The left flank, commanded by the viceroy, seized the heights but was soon pushed back off them. They retook the position and lost it a second time. Many generals were wounded, and the ranks were being dreadfully thinned. Even so, they closed up as the dead were replaced. Then, finally, at around two o'clock in the afternoon, just as we were launching a final effort, the cuirassiers seized the Great Redoubt. The Russians attempted to retake it a number of times. They made it as far forwards as the ditches but they were pushed back each and every time. The position was a redoubt in name only, the ditches were filled with corpses, the cannons had been spiked and roundshot had demolished the earthworks which had still been standing just a few hours previously.

It was now getting late. We were masters of the centre of the enemy line but, even so, the battle was not decided. Everything depended on what was to happen on our right flank. The marshal commanding that part of the field, encouraged by our success on the left, pushed forwards. It all took place so rapidly that the enemy was obliged to relinquish his position and fall back in retreat. It was then that the massacre became even more horrible. Some one hundred guns from the Imperial Guard artillery formed a battery in front of the Great Redoubt and swept the Russian positions with grape for more than two hours.[19]

No battle had ever been so sorely contested or a victory been so dreadfully costly for both sides.[20] An area around six square miles was covered with dead men and horses, spiked guns and the remains of burnt caissons were scattered about. It was butchery. The wounded from all the different nations gathered below the trees. They went without help and without the necessary means for existence. In order to get some water it was necessary to travel far from the field of battle. Any water to be found on the field was so soaked with blood that even the horses refused to drink it. We camped by the ravine before Borodino. The night was very cold and it rained a little. There was a dearth of everything. The Cossacks, who had remained perfectly inactive for the whole of this second day, moved forwards, now that the battle was over, and attacked the Smolensk road, wounding and pillaging a number of servants sent back to find forage.

The Russians had held on to the redoubts thrown up at the

point where the two roads to Mojaisk join. But, that evening, they abandoned them and during the night they withdrew towards Moscow, protected by a rearguard drawn up just in front of Mojaisk.

At dawn on the 8th of September, I visited the field of battle. I noticed that in many places the corpses were piled up one on top of another. The blood had formed into little streams and the roundshot and canister so covered the ground that they resembled hail in the aftermath of a terrible storm. In a number of places, primarily those which had been more exposed than others, and in front of our batteries, there were so many roundshot, shells and canister that it seemed as though the ground had been transformed into a kind of chaotic arsenal in which piles of roundshot had been knocked over and containers of canister scattered here and there. I could not see how a single person could have escaped. Yet I was even more amazed when I visited some of the ravines and made my way to the bottom of these little valleys. So many shells had rolled there that it was simply beyond comprehension and the sight had to be seen to be believed. I swear that I myself first thought that the shells must have been stored there and I could barely persuade myself otherwise. I had never seen anything like it before. I stood there like a person amazed, someone who didn't dare believe his own eyes. This place drew me back a number of times. I felt extremely sorry for all the miserable wounded who, as if following some instinct, had dragged themselves to these ravines in the hope of at least being out of the wind. These unfortunates hadn't received any help and were asking to be put out of their misery. There were so many wounded that there was no room in the dressing stations. Those who couldn't drag themselves away from the battlefield stayed where they were, exposed to be trodden underfoot by the horses or crushed by the wagons. Almost all of them would die from their wounds or out of misery. I saw a French soldier who had had his leg largely carried off by a roundshot, though it remained attached to him by a thin piece of skin. I saw him cut it away with his sabre so that he could drag himself along a little better and, I suppose, look for a peaceful corner in which he could die. He came over to a fire which my soldiers had lit for me and I had him made as comfortable as possible. Some other wounded saw this and began to drag themselves over too. I noted that, among their number, there was a Russian sergeant who had had both his thighs smashed and who spoke a little French. He had been a prisoner in France and had been at Tilsit.[21] My camp was soon overflowing with wounded and we had to seek out another spot. My servants and orderlies complained that I was being too charitable. They carried off the firewood we had collected and so these unfortunates found themselves once again abandoned.

I examined the field more closely and saw that an attack by our left would have been nearly impossible and, had it been attempted, it would have cost us dearly. Whilst I was out making these notes and observations, my cook had cut a steak from the corpse of a horse and presented me with it upon my return. He had also prepared some broth to go with it (for lack of bread). I found it excellent, and devoured the whole lot.

At around two o'clock in the afternoon we set out to pursue the enemy. We caught up with their rearguard at around five o'clock. They were positioned at a village on the Mojaisk road. There was a great deal of firing and a few guns opened fire. We camped on the road on the far side of the village. We lacked for everything, there wasn't even any water to be had. The Russians had, as they withdrew, destroyed most of the wells and the concentration of so large a body of men and horses in just one spot meant that any water remaining in any untouched wells was quickly consumed. By now it was very cold at night and the only firewood we had was that salvaged from the houses we destroyed. The village itself quickly disappeared in a few minutes.

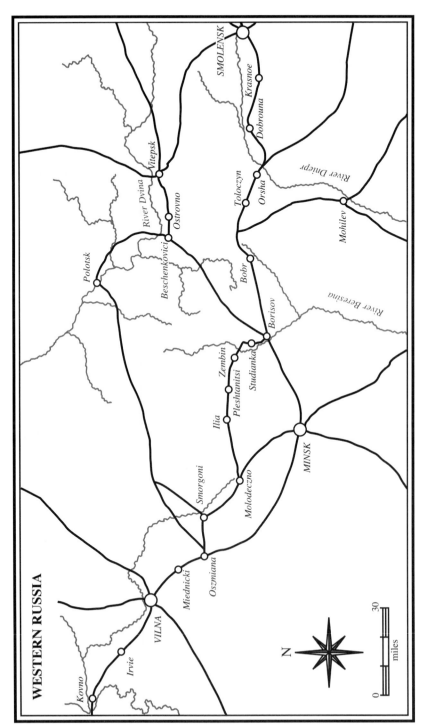

Map 1: Western Russia in 1812, showing the route followed by the main body.

On the 9th of September we continued our march towards Moscow, passing through the little town of Mojaisk.[22] It is the chief town in the district and is built on a hill overlooking two very wide and open plains, one being slightly more elevated than the other. I noted a very fine church which had not quite been completed.

The town was full of Russian wounded, whom the Russian army had been unable to take with them. We also came across many more spread out along the road. Many had seemed to collapse and die en route and the Russian rearguard had carried them over to the ditches, covered them with some earth and planted a cross on top of the mound.

Our vanguard was in action for much of the day. We camped near a village which was some nine miles from Mojaisk. The night was again cold and the wind was so strong that it made for a most uncomfortable experience.[23]

We had stabled our horses in a house in which we found, laid out on the straw, a Russian sergeant and four wounded soldiers. Two more had died at their side but the occupants had been unable to move them out of the room. In any case, they looked upon them as though they were asleep and seemed unperturbed to be with corpses, behaving as though they were instead with comrades who were still alive and in good health. We had the corpses buried in the garden and, following their tradition, turned their heads to face eastwards and placed a two-barred cross over their graves. The army was still not receiving any bread or any meat. Water was still very scarce and I was paying six francs for a bottle good enough to drink. Many horses were dying of thirst. Some had spent three days without even having a drink of water.

On the 10th of September the Orthodox Church celebrates the feast of Saint Alexander, the patron saint of the Russian emperor. We set out at eight o'clock in the morning. The vanguard was again in action for much of the day. We went from one position to the next, being fired on by enemy cannon and making little headway. So, by the time night fell, we found that we had only advanced some thirteen miles. We marched through Shelkovka and made camp close to the village of Krymskiy. This was on a plain covered in sand and dust. We spent the night in a ravine just beyond the place where all the muskets had been piled. There we were sheltered a little from the north wind, which was strong and bitterly cold. Famine continued to ravage our army and even horse meat was becoming rare. It could be obtained if it was half rotten, or bought for an exorbitant sum. Bread was not to be had for any money – it simply did not exist.

On the 11th of September, the Duke of Treviso, Marshal Mortier, had me called in and he gave me the order to take three hundred Fusiliers and to advance on the villages of Gholovko and Yakshino. Looking at our maps, it seemed that these two places were situated some ten miles from the place where we then were. We were ordered to bring back as much food as could be found and collected there.

Now, it is easy to conceive that such a mission would be difficult. We would have to advance through forests and swamps, and would have to do so without guides, using just a little sketch I had hurriedly made whilst looking at the marshal's map to help us. We might even encounter the enemy. All this was of great concern to me. The marshal encouraged me and had one of his aides-de-camp sent to accompany us. When word was made known in our camp that I was to lead the mission, everyone wanted to be part of the expedition and I had at least a hundred more men than I had initially been ordered to take with me. I had my men drawn up and informed them that we were to march against the enemy. We set out, guiding our progress by the direction of the wind and by following a little stream which I had stumbled upon in the woods. After marching for around six miles, I had the troops rest. I had two scouts, evidently Polish Cossacks serving in our army, brought to me. They informed me that a Russian division of around 1,800 regular Cossacks had just entered the villages we were marching on. They also told me that the woods extended to within a pistol shot of the local chateau and that it would be necessary to cross a river which cut through a field in order to get there. I hesitated for a moment, wondering whether, with so few men under my command, I could attack a division of cavalry but, remembering the misery which reigned in our division, and that the woods could afford us some protection (as the horses could only advance through them in single file), I had the men advance. I encouraged the men, telling them of my confidence in them and animating them with the desire to involve themselves in a daring exploit.

When we reached the edge of the wood, I sent a small vanguard forwards to seize the bridge. They were under orders to hold the position and to open up a constant, harrying fire on the village. The Cossacks mounted and, in some confusion, drew themselves up in the field just on the edge of the village. To push them back, I picked out a detachment of sixty men and had thirty sent forward as skirmishers and the rest deployed as though they would cut the Cossacks' retreat. This ruse worked as I expected it to and the Cossacks wheeled about. I had some of my men pursue them beyond the village.

I left the battalion at the edge of the woods and I sent the non-commissioned officers and officers into the village in order to collect the bulls, cows and calves, and the bread and flour, and have them brought to the woods. There the food was divided up for transport. There were some twenty bulls and cows. I had the poultry and the flour placed on a wagon and much of the bread was distributed amongst the men, along with a good ration of brandy. I also set aside a nice barrel for the marshal. Each soldier was ordered to carry as much flour as he could. Some packed it into their knapsacks. Others carried it in sacks, but everything was done in the utmost order.

The lord of the manor spoke perfect Latin and he thanked me

A sketch, by Faber du Faur, of a wagon carrying supplies. Vionnet took wagons such as this into Russia but lost them all in the retreat. (Courtesy of the Ann S.K. Brown Collection)

for the care I took to preserve order. We set off on our march back to camp and we were there just as night fell, without having lost a man.

Our entry back into our encampment was the cause of something like a real celebration. All the regiments had some meat, some flour and some brandy. The soldiers spent some of the night butchering the cattle, making soup and pancakes, and singing. I received a number of compliments from the marshal himself and I was praised to the skies by the soldiers themselves. But the senior officers were far from content and, instead of being grateful for the service I had performed, made their discontent only too obvious that I, who was always being assigned to such enterprises, had been selected for this mission. It was perfectly obvious to me from experience that few are interested in being selected when the success of a mission like this is in doubt, making excuses that it is not their turn, etc. Afterwards, when the mission has been a complete success, it is another matter entirely and everyone bemoans the fact that they were not chosen, despite having made it clear that they were available. This is all nonsense of course, and the fact is that a great many officers prefer to remain in the camp and not risk their lives or their reputations in a mission in which success hangs in the balance. In any case, the reputation earned in such affairs is often transitory and negligible.

These observations may be discouraging, but they are worth repeating so as to accustom young officers to coping with the vanity of others, not to forget their own modesty and to, on occasion, make it seem as though one is not worthy of such a command. Those are often the secret principles of success.

On the 12th of September we again found ourselves in misery and the soldiers were once more without bread. They were eating some broth made with rye. The region had been covered with wonderful crops but the tartars had continued in their habit of burning everything which they could not carry off with them.

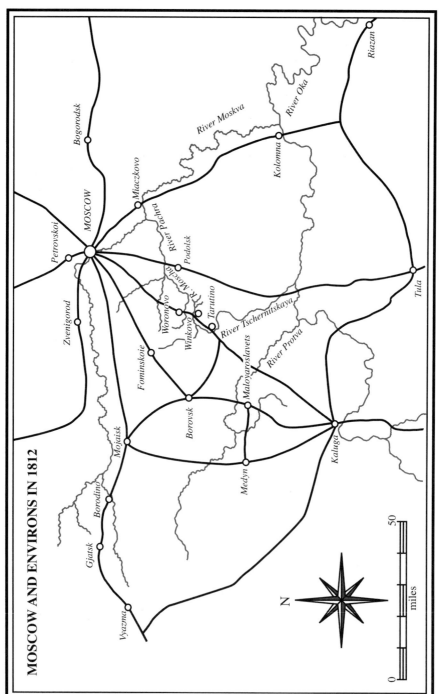

MOSCOW AND ENVIRONS IN 1812

Riazan

Bogorodsk

River Moskva

River Oka

Miaczkovo

Kolomna

MOSCOW

Petrovskoi

River Pachra

Podolsk

Tula

R. Moschla

Woronovo

Tarutino

Zvenigorod

Winkovo

River Tschernitskaya

Maloyaroslavets

River Protva

Fominskoie

Borovsk

Mojaisk

Kaluga

Borodino

Medyn

Gjatsk

Vyazma

N

0   50
miles

Map 2: The area around Moscow in 1812.

There were the smouldering remains of haystacks scattered about, giving off dark and noxious black smoke that obscured the horizon. We camped in a lane in the midst of a charming wood around thirty miles from Moscow.

On the 13th of September the Russians, having thrown up some earthworks on the Mountain of Birds, resisted our advance.[24] It was half-hearted, however, and they fell back after a few cannon shots. We camped near the chateau at Azintzodo [Asakovo], positioning ourselves in a small field behind some woods.

Moscow

On the 14th of September, the day on which the exaltation of the Holy Cross is celebrated, the Russians sent forward an emissary to parley with the emperor and to tell him that they were evacuating the city and that, after two hours, we might enter. The Russians asked that the emperor might take good care of the ancient capital of their empire. I received the order to position my battalion at the front of the column, just as had happened at Glubkoe, and to carry out the same functions as we had there until a commandant could be appointed. We would be under the orders of Marshal Mortier, the Duke of Treviso.[25]

I led my battalion to the Government Square[26] and we camped there. The marshal was lodged on the square too, staying with an apothecary whose house was on the corner of a street opposite the Governor's Palace. This man spoke French and seemed very intelligent. A young man who worked for him spoke Italian. These two were my chief sources for the initial information I gathered on the city of Moscow. I subsequently relied on information provided by the steward of a large mansion in which I lodged and which was located very close to the square. I busied myself with placing sentries and guards on all the public buildings, on warehouses containing food, on the Stock Exchange and the bank, and on the orphanage of the

An artist's impression of how the French entered Moscow. The troops did march in, bands playing, but the city was practically deserted and most of the inhabitants had fled. The fire, of course, started later and was initially put down to careless plundering by French troops. (Courtesy of the Anne S.K. Brown Collection)

A Fusilier-Grenadier on sentry duty in the ruins of one of Moscow's suburbs, as drawn from life by Albrecht Adam. (Author's collection)

innocents. This latter forms a huge complex and includes a number of vast warehouses. The rest of the division was lodged in the Kremlin and in a street called The Bridge of the Marshals.

The Great Fire

The first thing to strike me upon entering Moscow was the look of complete dejection on the faces of the few people who remained in the city. I saw many who were actually reduced to tears. There was a silence which prevailed and all the streets were empty. All this combined to make one pensive.

I had acquired a few bottles of wine[27] and a morsel of bread and, after eating a little meat, I set out with a number of soldiers to patrol the streets. I did this with the intention of becoming more familiar with the city and also to prevent any kind of disorder. I found that tranquillity reigned everywhere and we did not meet a single French soldier.[28] Just as we were entering the square again, as the sun was going down, I saw a very badly dressed man carrying a shotgun. He was trying to make his escape but I had him pursued and brought back. I interrogated him, using a Pole who was with us, and who spoke Russian and French, as an interpreter. He swore that he had been condemned to the galleys for life but that, before leaving, the city governor had released everyone and given them their freedom. My adjutant also informed me that a few of our soldiers, upon entering a building to buy some wine, had stumbled across a dozen of these characters hidden in the house. They were all well armed. I had a search carried out and a large number of these men were arrested and kept under guard. They were placed in a house which was next to the guard house. As night fell, I had patrols sent out continuously in all directions. I felt that these precautions were necessary so that the tranquillity of those inhabitants remaining in the city might best be assured. In no way could I have foreseen the impending catastrophe which would destroy this beautiful and fascinating city. Indeed, I thought that I was only protecting it against French troops and not defending it from its own citizens. I could not predict, or even imagine, that a modern people would have so much anger within them so as to be able to destroy their own city in order to deprive an enemy of the resources that were to be found there. It was the Muscovites who set this extraordinary example, one which will, no doubt, be followed by a great many imitators.

However, I must now return to those appalling events which saw the destruction of one of Europe's most beautiful cities, and describe what happened. I will restrict myself to what I saw with my own eyes, and whatever interpretation might be given to what is written here is for others to decide. The facts which I set down here are just that: facts. I am free from any particular bias, and I have no ulterior motive in writing what you see before you. If, by chance, these notes one day fall into the hands of some historian, he could make use of them with the assurance that they are extremely reliable.

Around midnight, I visited the outposts that I had established around the city. Arriving at the one just by the Stock Exchange, I noticed that there was a lot of dense smoke but couldn't see any flames. The officer in charge of the post said that he'd seen something similar happen earlier, but as all the city gates were closed, he thought that it must be some fluke of nature and nothing to do with the army. Whilst we were talking we took a closer look at the source of the smoke and it was then that I saw a flash of flame. I ran back to the square and ordered a hundred men to follow me, meanwhile placing the rest of the battalion under arms. Even though I'd only been away a matter of moments, when I got back I found that an entire house was now engulfed in flames and that the fire was spreading. I sent word to warn the marshal and he ordered that the pumps be found and that other precautions be taken to prevent the fire from taking hold. There wasn't much wind and we thought that the fire wouldn't make much progress. But we had our hands tied because we couldn't find any pumps, and because the gates were locked and we lacked the means to break them open. I immediately confirmed that the area that was on fire was relatively isolated and that only this part of the city would be affected. Only then did I manage to collect a few individuals and, together, we broke down a door and penetrated into the area in which the fire had taken hold. It would have been very easy to put the fire out had we had the pumps. But one of the men who I had with me, speaking in Italian,[29] said that there wasn't a pump in the entire city and that the governor had taken them away with him. He also told me that he thought the governor had given orders to burn the city and that this was to be done by men released from the prisons. I warned the marshal[30] about all of this and busied myself with measures designed to stop the conflagration from spreading further. I thought that by demolishing a little house which was being used as a shop we might prevent the fire from reaching any further and so we set to work with some twenty Fusiliers, a dozen inhabitants and myself. We were busy with this work when the marshal rode up to find out what was going on. He saw that we were doing what we could to prevent the evil from spreading, but he could not believe that it had been the Russians who had started the fire. He went off, and we carried on with our labours. I made sure that the doors to the Stock Exchange were firmly closed and that none of our men had been there. I found a few people inside the building who confirmed this was the case.

After four hours of incredible struggle and effort we managed to pull down the little building. I then thought it would all be over in a matter of hours and that the damage would be restricted to some of the peripheral and largely unimportant buildings around the Stock Exchange.[31] I was exhausted and could barely keep myself upright. I went back to the square where we were camped and managed to sleep for about an hour and a half. I was woken to be told that the fire had taken hold in a house which was on the other side of the Stock Exchange and that the wind was blowing the flames towards that building. I set off at once for the scene. Some of the inhabitants joined us as we sought to quell this new fire, making superhuman efforts. It was getting towards noon when, nearly exhausted, we thought we'd done what we could and the fire had been brought under control. We were nearly dead from fatigue when we saw something more horrible still, something that can be barely imagined. The fire seemed to have taken hold in six different places at once and, as though nature was in league with the rascals who were attempting to destroy monuments built over centuries, a violent wind was now fuelling the flames and causing them to advance at astonishing speed.

French soldiers looting in Moscow, as depicted in a Bavarian print produced shortly after the events. There was alcohol, and luxury goods in abundance, but a dearth of bread and meat. (Courtesy of the Anne S.K. Brown Collection)

A sketch of Moscow in September by the artist Faber du Faur. (Courtesy of the Anne
S.K. Brown Collection)

*Some of the unfortunate inhabitants chose to remain in, or to return to, Moscow.
Here are peasants in smocks, and some women dressed in what might be the
abandoned finery so freely available in the desolate city.* (Courtesy of the Anne S.K.
Brown Collection)

The night of the 15th to 16th September was terrible. There was the noise of collapsing buildings coupled with the sight of a monstrous firestorm and the crowds of unfortunates who had barely made it out of the flames alive. It was a spectacle that can never be forgotten.

On the 16th of September, around noon, I received the order to rejoin the regiment. It was without regret that I left this forlorn posting which had nearly broken me and in which I hadn't been able to help those unfortunate people. I was greatly depressed, even more so as I walked towards the Kremlin. I saw that the soldiers had been permitted to take whatever they wanted from those houses affected by the fire. I saw them loaded down with their booty, all stolen from the poor inhabitants, and, on the pretext that they were allowed to take what they could from the burnt houses, they were actually stealing from everywhere.

On the 17th of September the wind suddenly changed and the fires began to advance towards the Kremlin. So the emperor left Moscow.[32]

Incredible efforts were being made to save at least some of the city from the fire,[33] but the criminals who had been tasked with starting this demonic fire rendered our efforts useless. I went to seek out the house of a colonel I knew and who I had met at Tilsit. I was instrumental in saving his house from being pillaged or burnt down.

On the 18th of September the storm, which had lasted three days, took on a fresh impetus and it became almost impossible to go out into the streets and squares. I was resting at a crossroads, looking at the tragic spectacle this city now presented, when I caught sight of a peasant in the courtyard of the house opposite. He was setting fire to some straw piled up against a wooden building. I ran over and we managed to save the building. I had the man seized but he seemed so calm, just as though he had been kindling a fire in his own fireplace. He was sent off to

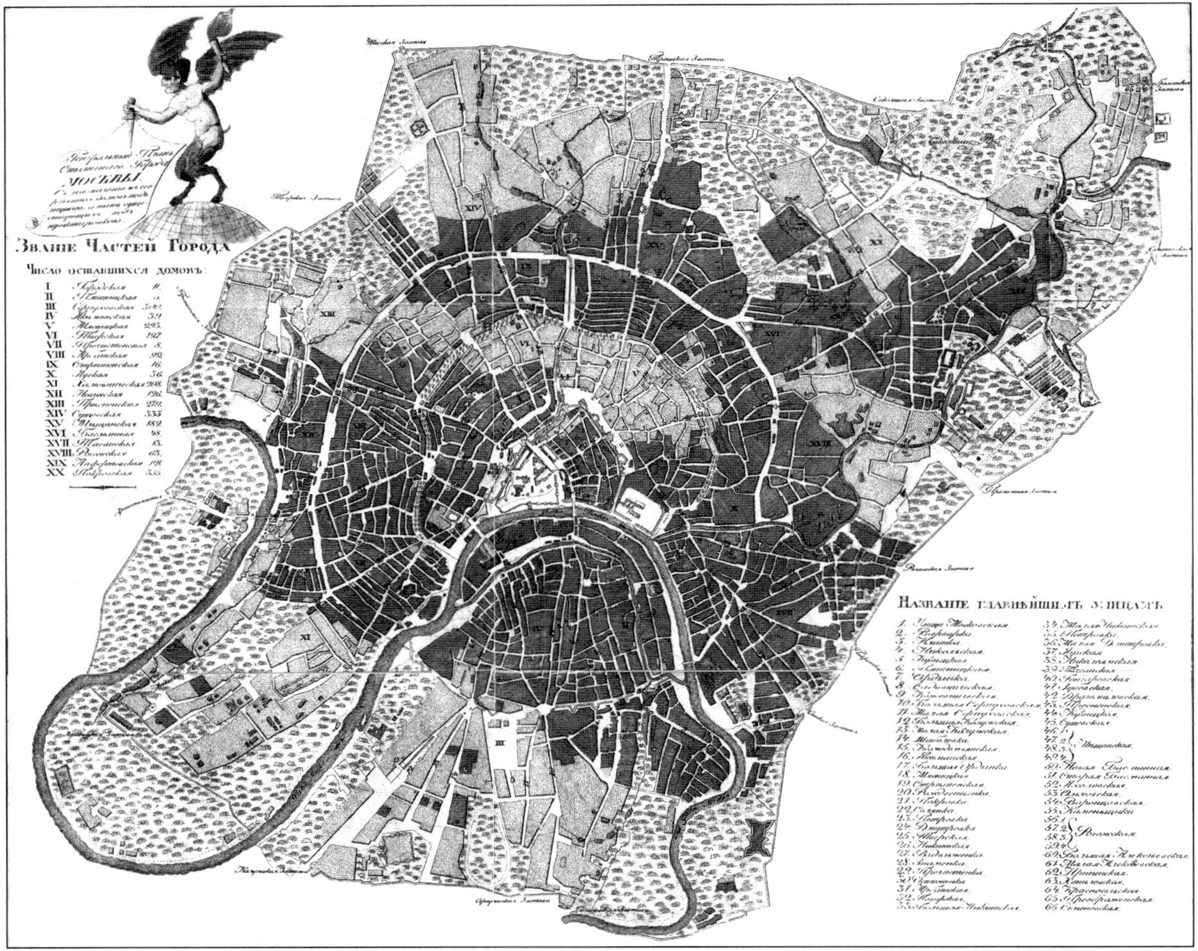

Map 3: A Russian map of Moscow, showing the areas destroyed during the fires of 1812.

prison, and witness statements were taken, but I don't know what became of him. A large number of these incendiaries were indeed taken and they were tried by a military commission. Indignation against these people was so great that the commission was given great power and did without much of the process and solemnity usually accorded to such proceedings. Some twenty individuals were caught red handed, and each one of them had been given the order to set fire to the city as soon as the French army marched in.[34]

Being obliged to return to the regiment, I returned to the house in order to pack. But I found that the house had been destroyed, and my servants, baggage handlers and horses were all milling around in the street not knowing what to do or where to go. They told me that soon after I had left they caught sight of a man setting fire to some straw in the house opposite. He had been determined to burn it down and my men found that the doors were firmly locked. They couldn't break in and the fire soon caught hold – the wind blowing it on to the house where I was lodged. They had had great difficulty in trying to get the coach and the horses out.

The storm continued. Soldiers were running through the streets, assisted by Russian peasants who had been recruited to act as fetchers and carriers as the soldiers pillaged.[35] The order was given for our men to remain under arms and to assist in the struggle to preserve the Kremlin, the Marshals' Bridge and the part of the city inhabited by foreign merchants. I was billeted at the Neledinski–Melinski[36] household, which had been spared. A steward, who spoke a little French, told me that his masters had had everything taken away. There was no bed for me and the entire house was devoid of furniture. No Frenchmen had been here before me. I thought that the steward had probably helped himself to whatever was left and would tell his masters, upon their return, that the French had taken it. The house certainly seemed empty. Then, one day, I asked him for a glass of wine but he told me there were only twenty-eight bottles left in the cellar. The very next morning my sentry told me that during the night he had seen the servant loading up some wine and other items on to a cart and making off.

The fire continued on the 19th but it started to rain and this dampened down the flames. The rain continued on the 20th and the fire diminished still more. On the 21st it was largely over, having lasted for just over a week since midnight on the 14th of September. The emperor returned to the Kremlin. Orders were issued that the pillaging must stop and soldiers found carrying pillaged items were to be arrested at the gates and made to hand them over. It was quite a sad sight to see those piles of expensive furs, fine embroidery and other precious items left there in the mud.[37]

I calculated that three-quarters of the houses in Moscow had been burned down. The Kremlin remained largely intact,[38] along with a few of the surrounding buildings, especially those by the Marshals' Bridge where we were based.

No sooner had the fire died out than I once more set out to see the city. At almost every step I was shocked to discover some new disaster. I was confounded by so many beautiful structures reduced to ash. Nevertheless, despite the horrors, Moscow still struck me as a charming city. It is one of the largest cities in Europe, with a circumference (including the suburbs and everything pertaining to the city) of nearly forty miles. The population is not in proportion to the immense scale of the city as there are barely 500,000 people resident.[39] The river Moskowa runs through the city; it is large and the city is named after it.

The city consists of four distinct quarters. The central district is that which is named the Kremlin and which is in effect a vast citadel in the form of an equilateral triangle. It is built on some heights and enclosed by high and impregnable walls. Within the Kremlin there are the emperor's palace, the house of the senate, the church of Saint Ivan, the arsenal, a large number of churches, barracks for the Imperial Guard, the mint, a stronghold in which the imperial treasure is kept and numerous other public buildings.

Upon entering the Kremlin, one is first met with the sight of a huge howitzer. Its mouth has a diameter which is one metre wide. Then there are six culverins which are mounted on static limbers. These resemble our own mortars and the longest of them is 8 metres long.[40] To the right is the arsenal and in front of you lies the palace of the czars. Before the palace there is a building which houses the palace guards. To one side is the cathedral of Saint Ivan the Great and, in the square between the church and the palace, the enormous bell usually known as the Bell of Moscow can be seen. It is said to be the largest in the world. It weighs 480,000 pounds and rests on the ground, left where it was put whilst the tower in which it was supposed to be housed is built. The foundations of that tower can be seen. The bell was cast following the orders of Czar Boris Goudonov in 1599 – a man who wanted to have something so extraordinary made that people would talk about him. He succeeded after a fashion because any foreigner who visits Moscow seeks out the bell, which, in addition to its size, is remarkable because of the ornate engravings that decorate it.

The imperial palace is largely unremarkable. The facade is quite regular, although the two sides of the building are less so. The formal staircase is superb. It is constructed from marble with a most elegant balustrade. The cathedral of Saint Ivan boasts one of the richest and most admirable appearances of any building in the world. The emperor and those officers who stepped inside were astonished by its appearance. The beauty of the sculptures, the elegance of the ornamentation, everything surpassed what might be found in even the most enchanted of castles. The walls are covered in gold leaf, the icons in the sanctuary are surrounded with diamonds and with pearls of the most extraordinary size and whiteness. Some are about as large as a pigeon's egg. We paused for a moment, lost in some reverie brought on by the sight of so much splendour. Our admiration was soon increased when we caught sight of the decoration which graced the ornaments used for the Eucharist.

The cross which is placed on top of the cathedral's dome is silver gilt and has a height of some nineteen feet and width in proportion. In addition to the principal dome, this cathedral has four bell towers and the bells within them are larger than any that might be found in Saint Peter's in Rome. They are so vast that they can't actually be swung – they are fixed to the walls on two sides and the clapper alone is left free to swing. When it is time for the bell to be rung, men are positioned on either side of the clapper and swing it so that it hits the side of the bell – the resulting sound is louder than that made by a cannon of the largest calibre. I counted sixty bell towers in the Kremlin alone. All of the domes of the churches, and not just those in the Kremlin, are gold and some resemble a kind of balloon held motionless in the air. The sight of all these domes when the sun shines upon them is such that our language simply can't convey the effect. The best place where one can enjoy such a sight is at the foot of the tower of the cathedral of Saint Ivan and from there one can look out over the entire town. It seems to me that a brilliant panorama could be painted from that spot.

The imperial treasure housed and guarded in the Kremlin contains a vast number of pearls, diamonds and precious stones. The weapons of Peter the Great are also stored here, and of particular interest is the sword that Peter wore at the battle of Poltava,[41] artefacts belonging to Catherine II and the trophies captured by the Russians during different battles.

The Kremlin was established by Daniel Alexanderovitch in 1303. This prince had been given the district of Moscow to govern by his brother, Czar Andrei Alexanderovitch.

The second quarter of the city is close by the Kremlin and is named Kitaigorod, or the city centre. It is sometimes referred to

An Imperial Guard caisson being transported out of the Kremlin. This image was drawn on the 17th of October 1812, as the army was preparing to leave Moscow.
(Courtesy of the Anne S.K. Brown Collection)

as The City. The word Kitaigorod translates as China Town and it is so named because the caravans which come from China deposit their merchandise here. China, however far it is from Moscow, nevertheless borders the Russian empire. There are a number of boutiques selling oriental merchandise in this district of the city. Many foreign merchants have also chosen to make their homes here.

The third district surrounds the two other areas of the city. It is called Beloigorod, or the white town. It has been given this name because the houses in this quarter are built from stone and have been given a coat of white paint. Lastly the fourth quarter, which is on the fringe of the city and surrounds the other three districts, thus forming an immense circle, is called Zemlianoigorod, or town of earth. It is believed that this area received this name because it was once ringed by earth ramparts constructed during the wars being waged during the reign of Czar Feodor Ivanovitch.

There are around thirty suburbs. Huge palaces are scattered amongst them and these can easily be mistaken for temples. They all have balconies, pillars, balustrades and other such ornamentation. Many of the houses are covered in cloth and the result is that fires are relatively rare, despite the fact that there are still a large number of houses constructed out of wood.

Moscow is the storehouse of the empire and a warehouse for all kinds of merchandise from Europe and from Asia. The Stock Exchange is an immense building and within its walls a vast amount of supplies are kept in storage, supplies which would last for a number of years. When I went into the building, I was struck by the huge quantities of sugar, coffee, cotton, Champagne, Bordeaux wine, Burgundy, oil, rum and other such things being kept there. I was particularly impressed by a timber yard, which I first mistook for a place where firewood was being kept, as it proved to be a stockpile of all manner of scented, exotic and unusual woods from the Indies. This vast wealth was all consumed by the fire. The resultant flames resembled a fireworks display, being blue in some places, white in others or a veritable mixture of different colours.

The educational establishment, which is located to the left of the Kremlin, is quite close to that place and is on the left bank of the Moskova; it is an extraordinary building and one which is particularly grand. It is also known as the House of the Innocents. For it is there that a number of children are brought up with much care and attention. The children are illegitimate offspring, those born to parents who, through poverty, cannot afford to raise them, or the orphans of military personnel who died in the service of their country. Within the confines of the building there is a public pawnbrokers where, at a very reasonable rate of interest, one can deposit all manner of items.

On the right of the Kremlin, as one draws near to the river, a very beautiful stone bridge over the Moskowa comes in to view.

The military hospital, which was once an imperial palace but which Peter the Great had converted into a hospital that could house 6,000 people, takes in the sick and treats them at the state's expense.

Close to the admiralty building is the extraordinary tower called the Sukareva Barreguia. It is very high and, at the foot of the tower, a boat built during the time of Peter the Great is kept at anchor. There is also a storehouse for brandy built in the shape of a rectangle. The entrance is through two folding doors which are placed opposite each other. The governor had had so much brandy emptied out that one could sail a ship in the courtyard, nevertheless such an enormous quantity still remained that it was possible for the entire French army to be issued with three rations per day from this stock for the duration of its stay – and much remained untouched even after our departure.[42]

I was particularly taken by a public promenade (known as the wall) which greatly resembled the boulevards of Paris and which was built on what once had been defensive works. The public baths are situated along this promenade and it was here, once upon a time, that people would bathe together. It would all be pell-mell, with men, women, girls, boys and infants all together without the least suggestion of shame or embarrassment. An Italian merchant who had been living in Moscow for many years showed me these baths.

I had to interrupt my exploration of the city because it wasn't especially safe to explore those areas which were now in ruins and because we were almost constantly on duty or on parade. These tasks took up much of the day. Although the necessities of life could be easily had, and were quite abundant, I thought that this style of living probably would not last. I therefore set aside around twenty large dried biscuits, three loaves of sugar, 25 pounds of coffee, some tea, twenty bottles of wine and thirty of rum or brandy. I had all these items placed in my carriage and carefully stored away so that they would not be damaged by the cold or broken by jolting.

That was all I was to take from Moscow. I had a cloak made from grey cloth with a fur lining. I bought the cloth and the fur from a French merchant and he made me pay a very high price for them. In addition, I bought a fur riding coat, an item which was incredibly warm, from a French officer.[43] I felt that, thus equipped, I would be ready for departure and that I was as prepared as possible for that which we were about to face.

I was in the middle of making my preparations when an emissary arrived carrying what seemed to be terms for the conclusion of a peace. This seemed to me, as well as to a number of other officers, a kind of trap designed to keep us in Moscow until the harsh season was upon us. The emperor fell into this trap with his eyes wide open.[44] He continued to have us reviewed, something which exhausted the soldiers, but failed to take the necessary precautions to safeguard our communications with Poland. Suddenly, the Cossacks assumed importance, whilst before they had been insignificant. They intercepted convoys and captured the troops who were acting as escorts.[45] And, meanwhile, the weather began to change, the nights were starting to get cold, the skies were cloudy and everything heralded the onset of winter, the most terrible season in the frozen north.

On the 9th of October orders were issued that each regiment should arrange to have provisions for six months. We collected an amount of grain, and of potatoes, which we dug up from the outlying fields. We also had vegetables, and everything else that might be deemed necessary. This order spelt disaster for those unfortunate inhabitants who had, until now, escaped from the catastrophe that had befallen their town. Whilst all these preparations were being made, those houses which were closest to the walls of the Kremlin were demolished and the ramparts themselves were secretly mined.

And yet there was something of a contradiction between these measures and some others, a contradiction which could not fail to elude even the most short-sighted. For, in order to throw people off the scent, Napoleon had established a theatre and put on Italian operas,[46] all the time affecting a most relaxed and untroubled appearance. He promoted a number of men in the army, drew up a number of decrees and seemed to be perfectly untroubled by the onset of the winter season.

A large number of prostitutes had stayed on in Moscow[47] and a few honest women, reduced by want to starvation, had been obliged to sell their bodies to whoever wanted them. So it was that these creatures were everywhere; many had established themselves in the surviving houses to the extent that they were now acting as the owners of these buildings, dressing themselves up in the finery which once belonged to ladies. They had obtained some of the luxurious clothing pillaged by the army, and received ingots of precious metals for services rendered. There was a distinct contrast between their behaviour, appearance and clothes.

I frequently came across elderly inhabitants who were literally crying because of the terrible scenes around us. I lacked the language to console them, but I gestured towards heaven and they would come to me, kissing my hands and leading me to the ruins of their homes where their families were dying of starvation and misery.

I took advantage of being sent out with detachments looking for supplies of food in the countryside to examine the region around Moscow. It is full of palaces and charming stately homes. Of particular note are Czaritsina, Kalomenskoi and Peterhof, the country residences of the emperors of Russia. Peterhof is around four miles from Moscow in the direction of St Petersburg. It is there that the emperor rests when he travels from St Petersburg to Moscow, preparing for his official entry into the latter city. There are also a large number of country houses which belong to private individuals. Curiosity would lead one to visit Astanchina, the country seat of Count Cheremetiev;[48] Petrovsky, which belongs to Count Razumovsky; Arkangelski, a palace built by Prince Galitzin;[49] Sirlova, the estate belonging to General Vissotsky and which boasts a pretty theatre; Lublino, which belongs to Mr Durasov;[50] then there are the estates of Countess Orlov, General Divov, and many others besides.

The most impressive country house is supposed to be Gorenki, belonging to Count Alexis Razumovsky. It is here that he has established his botanical garden where all known varieties of European plants are cultivated.[51]

According to some historians, Moscow was founded in 1147, although others affirm it was 1149, by Grand Duke Yuri Vladimirovitch Dolgoruky. The surname means 'long arm'. The city is built in the midst of a vast plain and this has been given the name the sacred plain. In effect, it forms an immense basin in which waters running from melting snow collect and so some of the greatest rivers in Russia have their source here. The Volga, which passes to the north of Moscow, snakes eastwards and flows into the Caspian Sea. The Dnieper, or Borysthenes, passes to the west of Moscow, then flows southwards and into the Zabache Sea[52] at Ochakov, whilst the Dvina flows westwards before spilling out into the Baltic Sea at Riga. All these have their sources very close to one another, very close to the border between the Tver and Smolensk regions. Another important Russian river, the Don, once known as the Tanais, splits into seven distinct branches and flows into the Black Sea or the Pontos Euxeinos. The source of this river is located to the southwest of Moscow, near Ocha.

Water is comparatively hard to find around Moscow, despite these rivers. This is especially true along the Moscow to Smolensk road. We often experienced a shortage.

The Russians have a number of things in common with the Greeks, and they follow the same religion, which is the Orthodox religion. Their cemeteries are usually located alongside their roads, usually in a location that is a little elevated or raised up. They are not enclosed by walls, nor even by hedges, and this lends them the appearance of those Elysian fields of the classics. They often irrigate them with rivulets or site them in cool places, so that the grass there is always green. They are usually round and ringed with trees which are planted quite closely together. Each grave has one, or sometimes two of unequal height. It is quite common to see a pine planted in the middle of the cemetery and this gives a most agreeable shade where one can rest during the oppressive heat of the hot season. It also serves as a shelter from rain during bad weather.

These places really are a fitting place of rest where one can be taken, leaving behind the passions which have tormented us whilst alive. By this means they have taken some of the sting out of death, and one can look upon death without fear or anxiety and welcome that moment when one will rest for ever in such a peaceful sanctuary.

Most of the trees that are planted in such holy places are native types, mostly being silver birches. These trees are extremely important here. They use them to build their houses, they make shoes out of their bark and even distil an alcoholic drink, resembling wine, from the tree's catkins. The space between the graves is taken up with a network of little paths which, because of all their little twists and turns, form a kind of labyrinth. I have seen marble, stone or painted wooden headstones on a number of graves. The friends of the deceased write messages upon them, often describing the dead person's virtues, and looking into the future when they too will join the dead there.

Just before I entered Moscow I saw a cemetery which was the same size as the Champs Elysées in Paris and which was open as a public promenade. I swear that I have never seen anything so extraordinary and this place left me full of admiration.

The inhabitants of Russian cities are generally dressed as those in the rest of Europe. The only exception is in winter when they wear overcoats made from different furs and hats from marten pelts, sable or astrakhan. In town shoes or boots are worn and, whenever Muscovites have to travel anywhere when it is cold, they wear very long boots (which come up to the middle of the thigh); these are especially thick and lined with fur and resemble the boots worn by our fishermen. The peasants, or, more precisely, the serfs, wear a costume which very much resembles that worn by the Poles or, perhaps more accurately, that worn by Asians. It consists of a long and rather shapeless smock divided in two at the waist by means of either a leather belt (worn on special occasions) or, on most days, by a simple cord. Their shirt has no collar, they wear underwear and, for footwear, they have sandals crafted from the bark of birch trees. These are attached to the leg by means of laces which are wound around the leg so that their footwear resembles that worn by the ancient Romans. In winter they wrap themselves in fur and wear smocks and underwear which have been lined with wool.

The Russians, despite living in a bitterly cold climate, greatly feel the cold. Each respectable household has a thermometer at the entrance to each room and the moment it falls to below 25 degrees [minus 28 degrees Celsius] nobody goes out and for all the time that such a temperature endures, the streets are empty and the public squares abandoned.

The houses in the cities, even those which are built out of wood, are very handsome and usually quite spacious. There are many, especially in Moscow, which are built almost entirely out of bricks, stone being relatively difficult to procure in this part of Russia. The houses of the peasantry are made out of wood, with the exception of a stove and a very small chimney. A number of planks are placed over the stove, forming a kind of bed and this is usually offered to visitors, being the best bed in the house. The bed is raised up and has a kind of bar to prevent one from falling out and on to the stove. A bench runs all the way along the walls of the room and in one of the corners, usually that opposite the door, there is a table. In the other corner there is a small barrier behind which is piled straw and this is where the entire family sleeps, all mixed up together with no distinction for sex or age. When there is a newly married girl living in the house, she is allowed to occupy the bed above the stove with her husband. The poorest of the peasants live with their livestock, be they cows or horses. The height of luxury for such people is to have two rooms. This allows the different sexes to sleep in different places, for it is then that they are able to raise a kind of couchette above the straw. That is the best that these people can aspire to.[53]

The exterior walls are constructed out of birch logs and these are laid one on top of another; the process is simple and the logs are only straightened a little where they have trouble meeting. Sometimes one sees cases where things have been arranged so that one log has its convex side facing out, but the log below has the convex part facing inwards. At the corners the logs meet and are bound together and notched in such a way as to keep them in place. This serves quite well and the walls thereby resemble our old-fashioned strong boxes, being strong enough to resist any of the world's earthquakes.

In order to insulate the cavity between the walls, the Russians make use of moss and so the walls are caulked in the same way as the hull of a ship. Sometimes the external walls are plastered either with clay or with manure, but generally the wood is exposed. The internal walls of those houses which have two rooms are often treated the same way but there is a major disadvantage to this way of doing things. The moss plays

92

host to a vast number of bugs, fleas and other unwelcome insects.

The openings for the windows are generally very small and for the most part there is no glass or paper over the opening but a mere plank that can be slid backwards and forwards, thus either opening or closing the window and letting light in during the day. This is how the peasants' houses are, those that can be found in the middle of the forests. It so happens that the constituent parts of each house can be numbered, then the house dismantled, transported and erected again in a new location.

The nobility is well educated and the towns are civilised. The arts have made much progress but many of the people continue to live as slaves. It is only in some of the imperial estates that there are people who have been emancipated. The form of slavery which exists here is not particularly onerous. There are a large number of merchants, apothecaries or workers who pay a large sum of money each year in order for permission to work in their industry. Others work the land and are not allowed to travel or marry unless they receive the written permission of their owner. When the landowner sells his land he has to specify the number of men, women, boys, girls, elderly, infants, horses, bulls and cows, etc.

Green is the Russian national colour and their particular favourite. The soldiers wear a uniform made from green cloth. The domes on the belltowers of churches are usually painted green unless they are golden. The shutters and the doors of elegant houses are painted in that colour. In addition, the statues of saints and the illuminated engravings always have some details picked out in that colour. Generally the Russians make much more use of colour in the arts and in painting than we do, and the result is that their work looks much more vivid than ours. In a sense, they resemble the art of China. The production of wallpapers which I saw in Moscow, and those examples I saw which had escaped the fire, seems to imitate the Chinese style.

We pay the earth for such papers and I have no doubt that the Muscovites pass off their own manufactures as those made by the Chinese, simply charging us extra as a tax on our luxury.

Baths are very common in Moscow and they are treated, much as they are in the Orient, as a kind of religion. The houses of the wealthy all have a bath room where the luxury and decadence of Asia meet the cleanliness and elegance of Europe. The bath room is usually divided into two distinct parts; the first is for undressing or dressing. It is decorated with mirrors and heated by means of heated pipes, and has a divan against the wall which is wide enough for one to sleep on. The parquet floor is covered with a carpet and there is usually a cushion or bolster, like the one we use in our carriages, made out of Morocco leather. The second area, where the bath is usually located, is usually tiled with marble. The bath itself is usually of marble or granite. It is usually raised above the floor and surrounded by a rail. When coming out of the bath, one descends some marble steps – these are usually white and very attractive. The bath has a bench around the inside where one can sit or even lie down, as it can serve as a kind of bed, and so one can bathe lying down. The flooring is heated to a temperature so that one can comfortably walk around barefooted. Above the bath there is normally a dome and on the ceiling of that dome there are paintings, with scenes of a voluptuous nature, as well as vents which can be opened to allow the steam to dissipate and fresh air to circulate.

There are also public baths. I visited the most famous of them and this is how I was treated. I was first of all introduced into a small but very clean room and I was asked to sit down on a small sofa. This was placed against the wall and ran along three of the room's walls. No sooner had I sat down, and without me being able to see where it came from, the room was filled with subtly scented steam. The temperature was increased so that the room became warm. A servant stepped forward to undress me, leaving me standing in my shirt and riding coat. He provided me with a pair of fur slippers and bade me enter the adjoining room. This room was hotter and the steam was much more dense. It was, however, unscented. There were a number of benches lining the walls and these were large and wide and upholstered in leather. The flooring was of the same material. Here there were two serfs who were entirely naked apart from a piece of cloth covering their private parts. A cord kept this cloth in place and this was tied around their loins. These two men were as tall as Hercules and had beards which descended down to their stomachs. They removed the rest of my clothing, lifted me up and, with considerable dexterity, carried me over to a bath which had been prepared in the adjoining room. There were in fact two baths in this room, one by the door and the other opposite. Next to them there was a kind of amphitheatre and this seemed to be where musicians could be placed. To the right and the left were heating pipes made out of some tropical wood. Water was occasionally sprinkled upon them and they then gave off a scented steam which was quite delightful. In the corner of the room were two camp beds covered with rush matting. The floor was of marble and it was heated so that it was a delight to go around with bare feet.

I had been in the bath for nearly half an hour when one of the serfs came over and began to comb my hair. He then began to rub my scalp with his fingers and treated my hair. He then rubbed my skin with perfumed soap and washed me a number of times. He then gave me a massage and left me to rest for another quarter of an hour. It was then that they both came in, picked me up and took me to the bed. There they rubbed me down with a flannel then one of them used a large woollen glove (which resembled a gauntlet) and rubbed me down several times. The second brought over some essences from different flowers and applied them to my body. I was then rubbed down with a smoother glove. I was then lifted up and stood in the middle of

95

the room where I was rinsed clean by having water poured on me three different times. I was then patted dry with towels, carried out to the adjoining room and reunited with the clothes I had worn upon entering the baths. I was then shown through to another room where the same servant presented me with the rest of my clothes.

I can confirm that I found the treatment extremely good for my health and I found myself extremely lightheaded when I emerged from the premises. I took a walk in the gardens and I carefully studied the house. The proprietor was a Russian but he spoke French and had travelled to and visited Paris. The house had suffered some damage but was still in relatively good condition. I had sentries posted at the property to ensure some security for his family and for his business, but I did not manage to visit the baths again.

It is sometimes the case that, when emerging from the baths, or from a heated chamber, the Russians roll naked in the snow and all this without feeling the slightest indisposition. It seems that this contrast between a great heat and the cold strengths the temperament and allows them to tolerate great fatigue and the most extraordinary privations.

One of the most enjoyable diversions for a Russian, whatever his social condition, is a ride through the snow in a sledge. A hill has even been raised up in order to recreate the experience – it is rather high, and, at the summit, a kind of theatre made out of planks of wood has been constructed. The summit is reached by means of steps leading up to the rear of the theatre. The descent is then made down the front of the hill, or down the sides. It happens at great speed and, in order to increase the speed still further, snow is laid on this artificial slope and more snow is placed on top of that. Water is then poured over these layers – it flows down the hill and freezes in an instant, forming a smooth surface and one as hard as crystal. They have small sledges which can comfortably take one person. They are designed so that the sledge can be steered with one's feet, so you can direct yourself towards your intended goal and reduce your speed if you feel that you are being carried away. The sledges are kept at the summit of the mountain and are pushed down the slope by an individual with such force that it seems that you are flying through the air. Their momentum is such that they are carried great distances into the surrounding countryside.

Before the road over Mont Cenis was built we had a similar system of descending the mountain. This means of descent was known as taking the plunge. Mont Cenis proved to be a dangerous place to come down like that, but here, in Russia, the worst that can happen is for the sledge to turn over and for you to complete the remainder of your journey travelling on your backside. The sledges are so low to the ground that it would be impossible to really hurt yourself. This diversion is especially popular among ladies and it has been known for clubs to form and for bets to be placed on who will travel the furthest distance, or on who will arrive at a certain place first of all. This entertainment can only take place in winter and would not suit our womenfolk at all. Their clothes are far too thin to allow them to tolerate the freezing cold which feels even colder due to the speed of the descent.

The Russian language is a Slavonic language and it is used in their religion and in all of their church services. The Russians tend to be religious, but they have retained some of the popular superstitions which date back to the time before they were converted. For them, Monday is an unlucky day. They prefer not to travel on that day, nor to undertake something of importance. The people seem to have their own particular mythology and the names of their divinities are scattered throughout the texts of their popular songs.

The verst is a measure of distance which equals a quarter of one of our leagues. Sometimes it is a feminine word, sometimes it is masculine. I don't know what the Russians themselves do in this regard, well that's all I know about the verst.

Whilst I was out exploring the city, Napoleon had collected up all the diamonds, pearls, gold and silver from the cathedral. He had also had the vermilion cross brought down from the top of the dome to Saint Ivan's cathedral. Apparently, this was because there is a proverb in Russian, used to show when something is impossible, which says 'that's as true as if the cross of Saint Ivan has gone to Paris', and he wanted to prove the proverb wrong. Or so they say. The Russians have another saying which has much currency and which says that the Kremlin has never been taken and never will be. They even say, when remarking on a particularly safe or secure place, that it is 'as secure as is the Kremlin'.

So it was that Napoleon collected all the trophies that could be found in the Kremlin and loaded them onto some twenty-five wagons. But, true to his character, instead of paying the army in silver, our pay was issued using Russian paper money.[54] This only had one quarter of its nominal value as one Russian rouble was being exchanged at 20 sous. Pay was set at twice the usual rate but this meant that the unfortunate officer would find himself being paid at half of his usual salary. For example, a captain should be receiving 200 Francs a month. He was being given 400 Roubles which, when exchanged against silver, brought in just 100 Francs.[55] Napoleon made a great deal of noise that he was paying the army double when, in fact, he had reduced its earnings by half. It would be hard to imagine a more blatant example of theft, and all that just as he was loading up wagons charged with gold. I have to refer you back to what I said at the beginning of the campaign – that the man was surrounded by cowardly flatterers who applauded even his most extravagant or ridiculous notions.

Retreat
On the 16th of October orders were issued to interrupt the gathering of winter supplies and to collect one month's ration of

flour and one month's ration of brandy. On the 17th a number of units were given the order to leave and the emperor proclaimed that we were setting off to destroy what remained of the Russian army and that we were marching on Tula and Kaluga, where Russia's only foundries are located.

On the 18th we received our orders to leave the following day. On the 19th we remained under arms from eight o'clock in the morning until ten o'clock in the evening and only then did we begin marching off down the Kaluga road. We marched through the city and made camp around two miles beyond the city's suburbs. We camped on a plain swept by an ice-cold wind. We could barely even light our fires, the wind was just too strong. Our firewood was blown away and the cooking pots were blown over. On the 20th of October our division made camp at Denisovo.[56] There was a little light rain during the night. On the 21st our regiment was assigned the duty of escorting the treasure, then parked just before Kraovske, at the corner of some woods.[57] On the 22nd and 23rd we remained in camp in the middle of some woods, very far from any habitation. On the 24th, the day on which the battle of Maloyaroslavets was fought,[58] we were camped close to Borovsk. Borovsk is quite an important town situated on a hill and split in two by a river which is fordable at most points, despite being quite fast flowing.[59]

On the 25th we were in the midst of an inspection when we were interrupted by some extraordinary cries.[60] A moment later one of the orderly officers rode up and urged us to cross the bridge as quickly as possible and rush to the emperor's help as he had been attacked by a pulk of Cossacks numbering some three thousand horse and he only had some fifty Dragoons of the Guard at hand to protect him. We reached the bridge just as he did. To me he seemed to be much shaken. His escort had actually sufficed to protect him from the enemy attack. A Cossack officer had recognised the emperor and had spurred

A party of Cossacks pass through a Russian village on their way to pursue the French. Their presence devastated the French, as these able horsemen prevented foraging for supplies by picking off isolated detachments and marauders. (Courtesy of the Anne S.K. Brown Collection)

forward with such impetuosity that he was about to seize him when a dragoon killed the Cossack.[61]

On the 26th of October, we remained under arms for the entire day and it was only when night began to fall when, just as we had managed to prepare some fires and some shelter, I received the order to march. The night was one of the darkest and we had to pass through some woods without paths and without being assisted by guides. After considerable worry and trouble, I arrived with my battalion at Borovsk. This town which, only as recently as two days ago, had been in perfect condition, was now reduced to a heap of ruins. It had been burnt to the ground and now only a few isolated barns remained standing. We camped in a park which lay on the edge of the town.

For some time the weather had consisted of a very thick fog, one so humid that one's clothes were quickly soaked and the ground became as wet as it does after the heaviest of showers. This made it extremely difficult for the wagons to move forwards. The number of such vehicles following the army was so considerable that the transport column extended eighteen miles. It is impossible to convey the disorder that this gave rise to. The drivers fought with one another to get ahead and whenever we came up to a bridge we sometimes had to wait up to twelve hours before we could get across. The vehicles had been given designated numbers, marking their position in the column, but even as early as the second day on the march there was such disorder that this had become meaningless. Those whose rank allowed them to keep a vehicle found that it was impossible to locate it, let alone obtain that which it was carrying and which they had great need of. This was one of the reasons that, even this early on in the march, there was a great dearth of everything. It was on this day that we heard, for the first time, the artillery caissons being blown up for want of horses to pull them. These were caissons belonging to the Italian army corps [IV Corps] which had lost a great number of horses in recent actions. There was a great deal of complaining about the fact that a lot of horses were being used needlessly rather than being used to save munitions which might be so essential later on. It was even remarked that a certain artillery general had formed, as he was leaving Moscow, his own convoy of twelve wagons, all pulled by teams of six horses. As we advanced a little further, we came across the debris of this artillery park and saw that parts of it were still on fire. It was a sad and very disturbing spectacle.

We set out once more on the 27th of October, this time following the route from Mohilev to Moscow. We camped quite close to Vereya, a pretty little town which, up until recently, had been preserved but which had now been destroyed by the Italian rearguard. We changed position a number of times that day and it was only around ten o'clock that we finally established ourselves. On the 28th the weather continued to be good, even though it was cold. We camped close to Mojaisk.[62]

The cold continued on the 29th and misery began to make its presence felt amongst us. Our food supplies were now exhausted and the surrounding countryside offered nothing by way of resources. A habit of stealing had established itself so strongly in the army and nothing was now safe. It was the case that we were obliged to carry provisions about our persons, and never let them out of our sight. Saddlebags were lifted from the backs of horses and cooking pots from the very campfires. On that day we camped between Gridnevo and Drovnino, just at the edge of some woods.

On the 30th of October the effects of disorders occasioned by the want of food and the absolute lack of life's necessities began to be felt. We camped at Gjatsk [now Gagarin], placing ourselves between the church and the town, whilst we waited for the army corps commanded by Prince Eugene Beauharnais to arrive.

On the 31st we marched for the entire day and, as night fell, we arrived at a village whose name I have forgotten. There was a most violent, and freezing, wind. We had all the trouble in the world as we attempted to light our fires.[63]

On the 1st of November we set out at four o'clock in the morning and we arrived at Vyazma as night fell.[64] We camped there. The cold, and the disorder, was getting worse. All the columns were mixed up together and the soldiers could no longer find their regiments.[65] The confusion reigned supreme and all the horrors that would fall began to reveal themselves to us.

On the night of the 2nd we arrived at a church surrounded by earthworks. There was a postal station and we made camp there.[66] On the 3rd we camped in some woods by the banks of a lake.[67] The waters of this lake were beneath the walls of a chateau in which the emperor was staying. We also spent the 4th of November there. That night, two of my horses were stolen. The camp was scoured and I found them both. But my regulation saddles had been stolen, and I never could find them again. That night the lake froze – to such an extent that one could walk on the ice the following morning.

On the 5th rain began to fall, and it was as cold as ice. The north-easterly wind was so violent that it easily penetrated to the marrow of one's bones. The ground was soon drenched with water and this almost instantaneously froze and formed a surface as smooth as a mirror. The horses could not keep themselves from slipping and the frost nails on the horseshoes were soon worn through. There was nothing to replace them and so keep the horses on their feet. There was nothing for it but to remove the horseshoes and let them do their best with their hooves. An attempt was made to wrap their hooves in cloth, but this very quickly came loose and fell off. We camped on the heights above Dorogobutz, quite close to a little belltower.[68]

On the 6th of November it began to snow heavily.[69] We camped close to a post house, ringed with palisades, in which the emperor was lodged.[70] The number of men and horses dying from want suddenly increased to extraordinary levels. At every step one came across entire convoys and these had to be burnt due to the lack of horses with which to pull the wagons.

On the 7th, I was on duty guarding the chateau where the emperor was housed. In the midst of all this misery, he had a generous amount of provisions and all kinds of wines.[71] We received a little flour and some beef or veal.[72]

Smolensk Again

On the 8th we camped close to a few barns which had escaped the fires. The emperor's wagons were halted here, some eighteen miles from Smolensk. I now saw the impossibility of saving any kind of vehicle and so I determined to abandon my carriage and the vast majority of my possessions.[73] I retained a portmanteau, in which I had a few shirts, a coat and a pair of boots. I had a few bags containing what sugar, coffee, wine, rum and bread I still had, and organised everything so that I would be able to withstand the cold and not succumb to starvation.

On the 9th we arrived at Smolensk. Initially we were placed in the same suburb we had been quartered in as we advanced into Russia.[74] But, the following day, we were directed off towards the Vitepsk suburb, somewhere on the road to Elnya. There we were joined by a detachment which had been sent from France and they informed us that the Russian army in Moldavia now occupied Volhinia [Volhynia].[75] Some of our officers thought that we would now take up a position here at Smolensk and would here attempt to stand and fight. However, quite besides the inconvenience occasioned by the extreme cold, no provision for feeding the men or horses had been made.[76] The men were reduced to eating horse flesh as these animals had died in vast numbers. So, despite the desperate situation, no one was looking after the soldiers. Indeed, they were being asked to perform duties which were strenuous even in times of abundance. Every evening one battalion from each regiment was sent off to a hill to stand guard and this despite the fact that they had no straw, no shelter and were expressly forbidden to light a fire. Such precautions were useless and only went to demonstrate the complete lack of humanity of those giving such orders. In any case there was no firewood for miles around.

It grew colder and the north-easterly wind continued. A small quantity of rotten biscuit was issued, as were some swigs of a local vodka which was more likely to make men ill than do any good. Despite such relief, a large number of men fell sick here. There was a great deal of hostility towards the officers, accusing them of being the authors of all our woes whereas, in fact, the officers were often the main victims.

On the 14th of November, with the cold now unbearable, we left Smolensk and camped some eighteen miles from the city in some woods.[77] The snow was six feet deep. The road was completely iced over, and the horses kept on slipping and falling. Many hundreds were then killed, and others simply died of misery. One of my servants, who was leading two of my horses, which were carrying some provisions, was murdered by some soldiers who stole everything they could and killed one of the horses. The other horse fell into the hands of the Cossacks.

Destruction at Krasnoe

On the 15th of November we slept in some barns at Krasnoe [Krasny]. During the night of the 15th to 16th we were sent out to attack a village [Malievo] then being held by the Russian vanguard. We managed to seize and hold the village. A large number of Russians were either killed or taken prisoner. On our side we had a few soldiers and some officers killed or wounded. I had five bullets lodged in my riding coat and was bruised twice by spent bullets. We returned to Krasnoe following this expedition, and spent the night there.

On the 17th we marched out in order to take up a position to protect I Corps, then acting as the rearguard as it arrived. What followed was a serious affair in which we lost a large number of officers and soldiers. The first regiments of Voltigeurs and Tirailleurs of the Guard were entirely destroyed – only a total of 120 men from both units remained. The two Fusilier regiments also suffered heavily.[78] I had two horses killed beneath me.

Just before Krasnoe there was a ravine crossed by a small bridge. That bridge was soon so clogged with wagons pushing forwards in their haste to get across, that it proved impossible to either go forwards or have them taken back. So it was that we were forced to abandon everything that remained on the far side. A young lady, very well dressed, with shoes made from white satin, was forced to abandon her coach and was now obliged to

105

continue on foot. She was carrying in her arms an infant of two or three months. Close by my battalion she lost her shoes, but continued onwards in bare feet, looking at her baby and occasionally raising her eyes up towards heaven.

Just at that moment we were hit by a large number of roundshot, canister and musketry. The woman didn't seem at all troubled, and perhaps even envied the fate of those who were killed and whose bodies now littered the plain. She went on, until I lost sight of her.

My left leg was badly hurt when my horse collapsed on top of it. The horse's leg had been carried off by an exploding

An unflattering, but not entirely inaccurate, image of the aftermath of Krasnoe by a British artist. Napoleon is shown being driven away in a carriage, whilst his troops gnaw at bones and the carcasses of dead horses. (Courtesy of the Anne S.K. Brown Collection)

shell. At the same time precisely I was also hit by a bullet in my right side which caused me some bruising. Once I Corps had passed over the ravine, we fell back through Krasnoe. Just behind that town the road runs through a hollow made by some elevated ground. The enemy had placed four guns and two howitzers here and these were inflicting heavy casualties. We did not have any artillery to drive them back and so we had to march forwards and run the gauntlet, there being no possibility of passing through to the left or the right of the road. Every one of the enemy's shots found its mark. The shells could not miss or pass over and every one of them killed or blew the legs off those in the way, wounding those when the impact of the shell was deflected by dead bodies. You can be the judge of the butchery occasioned by this battery of guns – everyone who witnessed it was discouraged and shocked as they watched the massacre. That evening, as night fell, we camped near a poor house in which the emperor was lodged.[79]

On the 18th, the retreat continued. On the 19th we crossed over the Borysthenes at Orsha and on the 20th we were at Dobrouna.[80] On the 21st we were at Oriba, on the 22nd at Kokanova[81] and, on the 23rd, we were at Bobr.

The cold was absolutely unbearable, and was especially so as the army had absolutely nothing to eat. A vast number of men were now dying from want. Their bodies covered the roads. Our bodies were so very weak that for much of the time the soldiers barely had the strength to light any fires, and often ate their horseflesh raw.

On the 24th we were joined by the corps commanded by Marshal Oudinot, the Duke of Reggio, which, only having advanced as far as Polotsk, had suffered less than ourselves.[82]

Crossing the Beresina
On the 25th of November, the army arrived before Borisov

[Barysau] which was occupied by the Russian army from Moldavia.[83] We camped by some heights looking over the town. The Russians had built some redoubts and positioned artillery within them. They occupied some entrenchments opposite the bridge. The town is built in a kind of amphitheatre below the heights which dominate the left bank of the Beresina. The crossing of this river is particularly difficult because of the marshy terrain on both of the river banks. A further problem was posed by the ice which would make any works begun in the river very difficult to complete. In addition, we lacked the necessary tools to undertake any sizeable project. Any such project would have to be completed under the noses of the Russians and with great speed – for the Russian main body could arrive at any moment. Then we would be surrounded, and the only outcome would be to face death, our weapons in our hands, or give in and surrender to enemies we had beaten so many times before. And then it would come to pass that we would end our lives in the deserts of Siberia.

On the 26th we were camped close by the bridge which was about a third of a mile long. We formed up in columns and, as there was a lot of wood around, we made several large fires. We then marched up river to Studianka [Studzjonka] where they were busy building another bridge.[84] We camped close by the place where the work was being carried out and as we watched we noted with concern that the work was going slowly and taking a lot of time. We listened to the firing coming from the far bank as the light infantry who had gone over to the other side sought to push back some Russian units. It was evident how reduced in numbers our corps were, and the regiments now consisted of very few men. The engineers worked all that night and, by the morning of the 27th, the bridge had been completed. A second one had been started, but this was never finished. The Guard passed over at dawn.[85] The emperor, the marshals and a number of generals were at the bridgehead in an attempt to maintain order. However, despite their presence and their efforts, the men were pushing their way forwards so violently and with such fury that the bridge collapsed a number of times.[86] This slowed the crossing down. We camped at the edge of some woods, on some heights, and surrounded by marshes. The night was a terrible one.

The battle of Borisov began on the morning of the 28th of November. The French army covered itself in glory. There was a cavalry charge which sowed a great deal of havoc amongst the Russian army and which threw them back into the town. We took a very large number of prisoners. At around the same time, Marshal Oudinot was wounded. That evening we camped in the same position we had occupied the night before. It snowed heavily and the wind was so strong that it blew out the fires, and

When it looked as though the French would be trapped at the Beresina, a number of regiments burnt their flags and hid their eagles. Whilst this scene is probably overly-dramatic, Vionnet noted that a number of colonels had the flags removed from their staffs and wrapped around their bodies. (Author's collection)

swept away the firewood. We suffered more than can possibly be imagined that sad night.

The crossing of the Beresina is one of the most remarkable events conserved in the annals of history. The army, exhausted by long marches, weakened through want of provisions and starvation, destroyed by the cold and nearly broken in terms of morale, nevertheless held together.

The position we were in was still one of the utmost danger and now everyone began to think of his own salvation. The bonds of discipline which held us together were now broken, there was now complete disorder. The stronger pushed the weaker to one side or trampled over them in order to get across the bridge. Crowds were pushing forwards to get across and it was necessary to now clamber over a mound of dead and debris even to get close to the bridge. A vast number of wounded soldiers, and the sick and women who were following the army, were thrown down to the floor and crushed underfoot. Hundreds of men were crushed when the artillery guns crossed over. The crowd surrounding the bridgehead formed such an immense mass that it covered a vast area and its movements seemed to resemble waves on the surface of the sea. As the waves swept forwards those men who were not strong enough to resist the shock were thrown to the ground and smothered by the crowd. The Russian army had by now drawn closer and a few roundshot and shell were fired into the midst of these unfortunates. Terror reigned supreme. A large number of people attempted to cross over by having their horses swim across. A few succeeded, but most were drowned, swept away by the ice or crushed under its weight. You could see individuals caught in the river and unable to get out. There they died, crying out for their friends to come and assist them.

The Polish division, which had been left on the left bank of the Beresina, was forced to retreat by the Russians.[87] It had great difficulty pushing through the crowd of stragglers and the debris and climbing over the piles of corpses. Eventually it made it across to the right side of the bridge but, as it was still being pursued by the Russians, they set fire to the bridge and thus abandoned to the enemy more than twenty thousand soldiers and servants, two hundred cannon and a thousand wagons. A few of the unfortunates made one last attempt to get across even though the bridge was on fire. They all died, either through being burnt to death or from falling into the water.

On the night of the 28th we were still camping at the place we had slept the night before.[88] Our shelters had served as a kind of

A moving and honest image of the wreck of an army. This sketch by Peter von Hess, later worked into a dramatic painting, captures some of the defiance, and most of the tragedy, of Napoleon's army as it found itself cornered by the River Beresina. (Courtesy of the Anne S.K. Brown Collection)

The crossing of the Beresina, as drawn by a participant. The reality and anguish of the scene are captured. Note the number of swimmers. Vionnet noted that, 'A large number of people attempted to cross over by having their horses swim across. A few succeeded, but most were drowned, swept away by the ice or crushed under its weight. You could see individuals caught in the river and unable to get out. There they died, crying out for their friends to come and assist them.' (Author's collection)

A more dramatised view of the same episode, but one which captures the terror and confusion of that November day. (Author's collection)

field hospital but these were then burnt down. We could not find any more wood. It seemed as though nature itself was now conspiring against us. Large quantities of snow were now falling. The snow was being blown so hard by the north-easterly wind that it was drifting and the violence of the wind was such that its howling froze our very hearts. It was almost impossible to breathe. It was getting colder. You have no idea how we spent that night.

On the 29th I went down to the place where the bridge had been. The river had almost completely frozen over. A deathly silence reigned where once the noise of battle had been heard. I could see some Russian units were now positioned on the heights at Studianka, where we had spent the night of the 26th. The debris which had been abandoned by the French army covered the plain on the opposite bank and formed a most horrible picture.

We then marched off from the right bank of the Beresina, passing through a swamp where I believe I counted no fewer than twenty-four bridges.[89] We camped in some woods. On the 30th of November we camped close by Pleshtanitsi. This village had been completed devastated and there were absolutely no resources there for us.[90] On the 1st of December the cold intensified still further. The Cossacks rode through our columns a number of times. I marched against them with some fifty Fusiliers-Grenadiers and, despite the fact they were many times more numerous than we were, a few volleys by platoon were sufficient to drive them off. We camped at Slaiki.[91] Here there were still some houses, but these were burnt down.

On the 2nd of December we arrived at a place called Illia and established our camp by the bridge. The Corps of the Army of Italy,[92] which had been stationed here before us, had consumed every kind of provision brought by the Jews who had been selling food as though it had been worth its weight in gold.

On the 3rd of December we camped by the ruins of a place believed to be called Molodeczno [Maladziecna]. There we were

113

fortunate enough to find a house and we spent the night there.

On the 4th of December, at Markovo, the cold was even worse. On that day it fell to minus 21 degrees.[93] The sky was clear and there were no clouds. But the cold was so sharp that the sun itself seemed pale and yellowish. The men were now greatly weakened by hunger and by the cold, to the extent that they no longer resembled human beings. Rather, they seemed to be phantoms of the kind which terrify the imaginations of children in their nightmares. You could see them flit from place to place, intense and mad, staring straight ahead and saying nothing. Their hair and beards were covered with icicles which hung like beads of shiny crystals. Their faces were blackened by the smoke of bivouac fires and the blood of those horses they had devoured to feed themselves. Most of them were without shoes and hats

The defeated army streams towards Vilna, leaving behind it the Beresina and thousands of stragglers. (Author's collection)

Napoleon abandoned his army and returned to Paris, leaving Marshal Murat in charge. Here he is shown handing over command to Murat and being escorted on his way by a Neapolitan guard of honour, few of whom would survive the cold. (Author's collection)

and their bodies were covered with sores. Their heads were wrapped with animal skins which still bore traces of blood. Whenever they caught sight of a fire, they would throw themselves at it to warm their feet. It would happen that they would fall into the flames and that those sitting around the fire would not go to the trouble of saving them. So there it was that they perished, in the midst of the flames, and perhaps even fuelling the fire.

The camp we abandoned that day resembled a field of battle. It was strewn with dead bodies, as was the road we passed along. Sometimes, when we passed an abandoned fire, the men, who rarely had the strength to even cut any wood, sat themselves

115

down by the fire. As the fire died down, the men simply died where they were, lying down. Others arrived, seating themselves on the bodies of their comrades, only for them too to succumb shortly afterwards.

On the 5th of December we camped at Smorgoni [Smarhon]. It was here that we learnt that the emperor had abandoned us the day before in order to set out for Paris.[94] He left command of the army in the hands of the King of Naples. We were now marching in complete disorder. All the units were jumbled up and confused and we were making very little headway. The days were so short that we were having to march along in darkness. The cold was getting worse and worse. It is impossible to convey how the soldiers cursed Napoleon when they found out that he had abandoned them. The wiser officers believed that he had been obliged to act thus in order to save France, re-establish the honour of our troops and create another army capable of resisting the Russians and maintaining the allegiance of our allies.

On the 6th of December, at Soupranouy, we found some barns which had been preserved and we piled in, pell-mell, with men, horse and corpses all mixed up together and piled on top of each other.[95] There we came across the remains of the Neapolitan division and of Loison's division.[96] This had numbered twelve thousand men when it had arrived at Vilna but by now had been reduced to just five hundred or six hundred men. No sooner had it become clear that the emperor had indeed left, than most of our superior officers thought about nothing but doing the same. The colonels of regiments would wrap their regimental flags around their waists and hide the eagle in a place where the Russians wouldn't be able to find it.

By now famine and misery had reached new heights. You could now see bands of individuals, known as the Senseless Ones, and who were, indeed, driven senseless, slicing open the bellies of living horses, cutting out the kidneys, liver or heart and devouring them with indescribable voracity. All this whilst the

116

animal was still alive.[97] Others, who lacked knives or swords, attacked the flesh with their teeth, tearing off flesh and sucking the blood of those horses which had collapsed on the ground but were still alive.[98] Finally, I have seen, with my own eyes, men driven so mad that they cut at their own limbs and suck their own blood, famine and misery having reduced them from reasonable humans to a state and condition very much worse than that of wild beasts.[99]

On the 7th of December we camped at Rovno Poley. The temperature was minus 24 degrees [minus 27 degrees Celsius] that morning but, during the night, it fell and, by eight o'clock in the morning, the mercury in the tube had frozen. I had managed to keep hold of a pretty little thermometer and I now shook it and showed several officers that the mercury had indeed turned into something resembling lead.

The road was covered with a sheet of ice as smooth as glass. This, combined with exhaustion brought on by all our fatigues, and the lack of sustenance, meant that thousands of men slipped and fell and were unable to lift themselves up. A few moments later and they were dead. They would call out in vain for help from a friend, asking to be given a hand. But everyone's hearts were now closed to pity and, in such universal despair, even the most sensitive souls thought only of one thing – self preservation.

The road was covered with the bodies of the dead and dying. At every moment one could see soldiers who could no longer continue any further, drop down to the ground and there die. In truth, no one could spend more than five minutes on the ground before death took hold of you. Friends would be chatting together. One of them, now very weak, would say to the other, 'Good bye, my friend, I'm staying here.' He would then lie down and, just a moment later, he would be dead.

On the 8th of December we camped at Roukoni. That was the most difficult day in this long retreat. The few horses that remained with us died there. The road was covered with their bodies. We could no longer set fire to those vehicles we were forced to abandon. The Cossacks did not cease to harass us, for no sooner had we settled in to our camps than they arrived with their artillery mounted on sledges. They would then open up with canister. Almost all our soldiers had thrown away their muskets and those who still carried them were just too weak to be able to use them properly. From the 7th of December onwards the cold was so intense that even the most robust amongst us were completely frozen. Many of those who approached fires would collapse down before them and simply expire. There were large numbers of soldiers whose fingers consisted of nothing more than bone – their flesh had frozen and fallen off. Many had lost their nose and their ears. A large number had been driven mad and these, as I have mentioned, were nicknamed the Senseless Ones. This was the last phase of their illness, for they would be dead within hours. You might easily mistake them for men who were intoxicated or extremely drunk. They would sway as they walked and utter the most incredible phrases – such things as might make you laugh if you weren't aware that these things were the prelude to that individual's imminent demise.

The effect of the cold was similar to the effect extreme heat would have. The skin would blister and fill with a reddish liquid. The blisters would then burst and the skin would fall away soon after. You might understand the process by placing a frozen potato next to a fire – as it defrosts it almost instantly turns into liquid. That was how it was with our bodies. Most of us now resembled bags of bones, dried out skeletons in which the bones supported each other.

Despite the very real hazards involved in getting too close to the fires, very few of our soldiers had the will-power to resist the lure of the flames. You could even see them set fire to barns and houses in order to warm themselves.[100] No sooner had they warmed themselves a little than they fell dead. Then more soldiers would arrive to warm themselves and would sit down on the corpses of those who had already fallen. They would then die themselves, just a moment later, as though the example set by their comrades had gone entirely unremarked. I myself saw more than eight hundred dead bodies lying around the ruins of a single house.

Others would stand by such a conflagration and would get so close that when the flames blew towards them, they did not have sufficient dexterity to retreat and would thus be burnt to death. You could see bodies which had been half consumed by the flames and others that were still burning, such that they resembled torches which lit up the night, as though they were placed there on purpose to illuminate our disasters.

Vilna

On the 9th of December we reached Vilna. We had tremendous difficulty getting into the city because the streets were blocked with guns, caissons, horses and wagons. Most of these had been turned over and abandoned as soon as the Cossacks had appeared. We were to be lodged in some houses in the suburbs.[101] But no sooner had we arrived than a band of Cossacks appeared with two pieces of artillery and opened up with canister on the houses we were billeted in. We therefore had to sally out and drive them off. A regiment of grenadiers was positioned on some heights and lost three hundred men who perished that night.

The Vilna stores were immense but they were ransacked. Instead of organising a distribution of rations, the doors were simply thrown open so that some obtained everything they could want, whilst others got nothing. I myself was fortunate enough to purchase a dozen bottles of wine, some bread and some meat.[102] My stomach was, however, so tender and weak that I only managed to keep down a very small amount of soup. The wine was of great assistance to me for the rest of the journey. I took it as one would take cough medicine, taking it from time to time by means of a spoon.

On the 10th of December we remained in Vilna. It was enough time for us to wash ourselves, and trim our beards (which were long). We were covered in ash and with a kind of black crust over our skin – so much so that we resembled mulattos. Rumours circulated that fresh troops were due to arrive and that we would take up positions at Vilna.[103] Hope was beginning to stir within our hearts when, around midnight, we received orders to depart. A large number of soldiers elected to stay in the city's houses and streets, preferring to fall into enemy hands, or even be killed, rather than to once more expose themselves to the cold. For the cold was practically unbearable.

We passed through the town and were ordered into a kind of warehouse. We stayed there until seven o'clock in the morning. Then we set out along the road leading to Kovno [Kaunas]. We had scarcely marched a few steps when a unit of Cossacks swept down, robbed a large number of administrative staff and some soldiers who were driving wagon trains and took them all prisoner. However, as we continued to march forwards in good order, they did not dare to approach us. Instead, they rode alongside each side of our column, keeping a respectful distance. Neither side fired a single musket shot.[104]

As we came out of Vilna, and about three miles from the town, we came up against rather a steep hill and were obliged to climb it. Ordinarily the road was quite a fine one, but the excessive cold had turned the hill into a wall of ice which no wagon could surmount. The treasury wagons which had made it across the Beresina, and over countless other difficult obstacles, could not manage to climb it. It became necessary to burn all the wagons and the cross from Saint Ivan's cathedral, as well as all the other trophies which had been carried from Moscow, and all the emperor's household transports. The treasury's gold was shared out, more than five millions in total, to the troops escorting the treasure. Most of these appropriated the money handed to them for safe keeping and kept it for themselves so that very little was actually saved.[105]

On the 11th of December we lodged at Sismari [Ziezmariai]. Although the weather was horrible and the cold remained as bad as ever, we made good progress because we had managed to get something to eat. I had loaded my last remaining horse with all the provisions I had managed to lay my hands on.[106] As soon as I arrived in camp that evening, I busied myself with preparing something to eat. I had cause to congratulate myself for having taken these precautions because, at around midnight, they came over and told us to make ready to depart at once.

On the 12th of December we marched from one o'clock in the morning until noon and got as far as Jewi, where we hoped we would spend the night. All that remained of our regiment was billeted with the Hessian brigade commanded by Prince Emile of Hesse.[107] We occupied a miserable hut and were piled one on top of another. These brave Hessians had been reinforced by a company at Vilna who were now escorting their flags. I believe they had around one dozen standards and they were carrying them with much care and attention, so much so that they had not lost a single one.

One could only admire the conduct of this young prince, a man who never once quit his officers, shared their troubles, shared their privations and shared their dangers as though he was just the most junior amongst them.

Kovno

As night fell we received the order to depart and we spent the entire night marching. I have never felt so exhausted. A thousand times I was taken by the desire to lay down on the ground and finish it all, as thousands before me had done. It was then that I found that my religious principles prevented me from voluntarily cutting short my days. It was too cold to ride on a

121

horse and, in any case, I barely had the strength to clamber up into the saddle. All my servants had died and I only had a soldier who looked after my horse as well as he could and he, like me, had very little strength left.[108]

Finally, on the 13th of December, towards ten o'clock in the morning, we arrived at Kovno.[109] I was lodged with a private citizen of the town who received me very well and could scarcely believe all the disasters that had befallen us. We spent some twenty-four hours in Kovno. In that time they managed to pillage the treasury and the storehouses and the soldiers pretty much stole whatever they could find. They were even stealing the officers' portmanteaus from the backs of the horses they were leading. They would steal from beneath our heads whatever we were using as a pillow. Those who had survived the disasters in Russia resembled, more and more, a band of robbers rather than the remnants of a great army.

The Aftermath
On the 14th of December we recrossed the Niemen, leaving behind Russian territory. The state of our army was beyond belief, they did indeed resemble a mob of men without weapons and unrestrained by discipline, rather like a gang of brigands.[110] They pillaged and destroyed everything, were deaf to discipline and to their officers. A number of them were wearing women's clothing such as pelisses lined with silk, cashmere or other luxurious materials. They were in blue, vermilion or one of many other colours.[111] In place of shoes, they had wrapped their feet in cloth and bound them with string. Instead of hats they had the skin of animals and this had not been tanned. Many of them wore fleeces taken from sheep, their head thrust through and with the loose flaps tied around the neck. Others barely had any clothes at all and you could see their naked and frozen bodies rotting away. The central square in Kovno [Kaunas] was covered in the dead bodies of men who had died from the cold or from

drinking too much alcohol.[112] Many soldiers had not consumed wine or spirits for quite some time and, upon finding a warehouse full of brandy, they had drunk to excess. Some fifty men died and were lying in the square. We still had a few wagons and these managed to block the bridge, so that it was extremely difficult to get by. We should have crossed over the frozen river, it would have been comparatively simple as the ice was so thick as to be able to support a 24-pounder gun. The surface of the river wasn't flat like a plain, it consisted rather of a series of hills made out of ice, and some of them were around ten feet in height. It was snowing heavily. On that day, the 14th of December, we spent the night at Pilluvisken [Pilviskiai].

On the 15th of December we reached Wirballen [Werschbolowo].[113] We stayed there on the 16th and we were reviewed by the King of Naples, the commander in chief, and also the Prince of Wagram, the chief of staff.[114] It was still very cold on that day, in particular the wind was so cold that it took one's breath away. On the 17th we were lodged in Staluponen [Stolupiany or Nesterov] and on the 18th we reached Gumbinnen [Gusev]. On the 19th we were at Juterburg.[115]

This was the first town we had come across where there was anything available to eat. Our supper, which to us seemed like some magnificent banquet, consisted of a soup, a portion of beef, two chickens and four bottles of wine – all this for seven people. We had barely finished this simple meal when I was seized by a violent fever. This continued until the following day.

On the 21st I took some medicine and on the following day had some quinine. But, as my condition was deteriorating, I asked permission to travel to Königsberg [Kaliningrad]. On the 23rd I set out accompanied by the Surgeon Major. We were in a sledge which I had hired. We spent the night at Wehlau [Znamensk].[116] The following day, as the entire area was so covered in snow and ice, we found it impossible to make out any road as such and our driver just took us along what he thought

Some fortunate survivors escaping from Russia in a sledge. Vionnet was fortunate enough to survive Russia and to make his way unscathed across eastern Prussia in a sledge. (Author's collection)

was the most direct route. So it was that as we were travelling along across the fields we came across a spring of warm water and our sledge rolled over and cast us into the water up to our necks. We were pulled out but, as we were very far from any settlement, we soon got extremely cold. The two of us were like two blocks of ice. We stayed like that for nearly five hours before finally arriving in a village (which I have forgotten the name of). There I used the last of my strength to get out of the sledge and into a snowy courtyard. They rubbed my hands and face with snow, and then gradually defrosted my clothes. I was then stripped and two Jews came forward and rubbed me down with snow for more than an hour. This was done so rigorously that blood started to trickle out from the pores in my skin as they became unblocked. I was then taken to an unheated room. They dressed me and then took me to a room which did have a fire. Now only the tip of one of my ears was frozen, along with a toe on my left foot. My surgeon, who had had himself taken to a warm room right away, had died a few minutes later. I left the village, having generously rewarded my two Jews and those who had accommodated me so well.

I reached Königsberg and was lodged in one of the city's squares in a house which seemed rather nice. But my hosts were rough and barbarous people who deposited me in an unheated garret with barely a blanket, and asking me to pay 12 Francs for some broth and a glass of wine. They did call a surgeon, who made it clear that my condition was most critical but who, nevertheless, did volunteer to treat me. First of all he gave me a large dose of quinine and some sulphuric acid, which had absolutely no effect. He then resolved to try Königsberg's famous arsenic remedy, a medication which saved my life.

The regiment arrived at Königsberg on the 31st of December. The following day, the officers came to see me and to tell me that they would be leaving on the 2nd of January and that the entire army was withdrawing to the Vistula. Despite the state I was in, I resolved to leave with them. I managed to hire a sledge for 40 Piastres and agreed that I would be driven as far as Elbingen [Elblag].[117]

I set out on the 3rd of January 1813, being accompanied by just one soldier who would look after me. My driver was nothing more than a scoundrel who took me off my route, driving me into a village where he demanded a further 40 Piastres and threatened to turn me over to the Cossacks if I didn't hand over the money right away. I spent the night sleeping on a bench in a room which seemed to be within a customs house. I was so ill I could not even stand up. I did what

I needed to do in my trousers. I was now so sore that when I came to remove this garment the following day, I also removed what little remained of the skin on my legs. On the 4th I arrived at Elbingen. I was most fortunate to encounter the officers of the regiment and they made room so I could be billeted with them. I was treated by the household doctor and felt that I was starting to recover. I therefore asked permission to go on to Berlin to complete my recovery. However, General Roguet refused to allow this. I therefore remained where I was until the 11th of January, when I received the order to immediately make my way to Marienburg [Malbork]. I set out with two officers, and we had two sledges. The Cossacks were already occupying much of the surrounding area and as we approached the banks of the Vistula we found ourselves once more amongst them. We had to push on at once. I had our two sledges placed on the frozen river Vistula, remembering that there was a canal which connected the river to Elbingen. The local horses were capable of trotting along on the ice, whilst those ridden by the Cossacks found the going much harder. They did pursue us, however, for around an hour, riding along on both banks of the river, shooting at us with pistols but with their shots not being able to reach us.

After a most trying journey, especially for an invalid such as myself, we arrived back at Elbingen at around eight o'clock in the evening. The following day the unit received orders to leave Elbingen. We found a cart which we purchased and we were given some horses. We made it to Marienburg during the night of the 12th of January.[118] We were poorly lodged and we only managed to obtain some thin soup made out of beer and some eggs. My travelling companions had frozen feet but their stomachs would have been made more comfortable if they could have enjoyed a more succulent meal.

On the 13th of January the army continued its march and reached Dirschau [Tczew]. It was announced that the troops would then continue to Posen [Poznan].[119] However, we could not find any shelter in the town and so I determined to continue onwards to Starogard [Starogard Gdanski], where we were billeted with a doctor who treated us really rather well. He informed us that the Cossacks were blocking the road to Posen and that it was dangerous to travel that way without an escort. This information persuaded me to change my plans and I resolved to follow the route which ran closer to the coast. Following this road would mean that I would be less exposed to the Cossacks and that there would be more by way of resources. So, as a consequence, we followed that road, reaching Alt-Kirschau [Stara Kiszewa], a squalid little village, where we spent the night of the 14th.

Although it was still very cold, there was, for us, a marked difference in temperature, to such an extent that it seemed like spring. We spent the whole day in our cart with no coverings other than a simple coat – and we didn't feel the cold. We found that there was nothing to eat at Alt Kirschau. On the 15th of January we were at Konitz [Chojnice]. On the 16th of January we were at Jastrow [Jastrowie] and on the 17th at Schonlanke [Trzcianka]. On the 18th we reached Driesen [Drezdenko] and on the 19th of January we were at Friedberg [Strzelce Krajeńskie]. On the 20th we reached Landesberg [Gorzów Wielkopolski] where we came across the two regiments of Tirailleurs and Voltigeurs which had been sent on from Paris. They had superb bands of musicians, all tremendously turned out.

On the 21st we were at Kustrin [Kostrzyn] and arranged things so that we could stay there on the 22nd. We were billeted with an apothecary on the corner of the town's squares.

In Berlin
On the 23rd we were at Müncheberg and the 24th, Dahlewitz. On the 25th of January, we reached Berlin.

We had encountered the King of Prussia close to Müncheberg. Apparently, he was going to Breslau [Wroclaw] in

Silesia. At Berlin I lodged with a Mr Simon, an architect living in Frederick Strasse. There I was treated with a great degree of courtesy and humanity and I spent the 26th and 27th of January there.

On the 28th I spent the night at Wittenberg. I won't continue my description of the scenery around here because I have already described it when I previously passed through the region.

At Leipzig, on the 29th, I learnt that all the officers had received orders to make speed and travel to Paris post-haste. I spent the 30th of January in Leipzig, hoping to find Colonel Bodelin, whom I believed to be still here. On the 31st I was at Naumburg and it was here that we sold our cart horses. On the 1st of February we were at Erfurt, on the 2nd at Eisenach; on the 3rd at Vacha; the 4th at Fulda. On the 5th we were at Schluchtern, the 6th at Hanau and the 7th at Frankfurt. On the 8th we were at Mayence [Mainz].[120] I was lodged at the Hotel of the Three Crowns, that's where the stage-coaches stopped. I stayed there until the 13th, when I left for Paris, where I arrived on the 18th of February at one o'clock in the afternoon.[121]

The malady which had affected me was a kind of inflammatory, debilitating fever [ataxiadynamia]. It had been purged from me but left me feeling terribly weak, especially in my lower body (to such an extent that they feared for my life, or at least feared that my health would be damaged for some considerable time). The methods by which the fever had been destroyed had been so violent that my organs had suffered as a result. My legs and feet were swollen in a most terrifying manner. It was not until the 20th of March 1813 that I was able to pull on my boots. I was still quite sick on the 20th of March when I went to Panthemont [Penthemont] to re-enter the service.[122]

The condition I was in can perhaps be easily imagined. The soldier who had been accompanying me had remained behind, sick, at Mayence. I did not have any horses, and had no equipment; in fact I had nothing. I would have to replace everything in order to be able to take part in the campaign which was about to begin. Despite the injustice committed against me by the fact that I was not awarded any kind of advance, I was determined to participate in the campaign and so I did what I could to prepare myself so that I might be ready to leave at a moment's notice. First of all I acquired two fine horses, both with regulation saddles and everything that might be necessary. However, my feet were still swollen and a kind of inflammation troubled the rest of my body. That was the condition I was in when I once more set out. The remarkable thing was that, instead of tiring me, as everyone thought it might, the journey hastened my recovery and led to the perfect re-establishment of my health.

In Paris

I was still in the condition that I alluded to above when, on the 30th of March 1813, at around four o'clock in the afternoon, I received my marching orders which stipulated that I should leave the following morning before the break of day. I had to hastily arrange my own affairs, and look to those of the regiment. I spent the whole night doing so. I then set off with the battalion of Fusiliers-Grenadiers that I still commanded. On the 31st of March, at six in the morning, we halted at Bondy and then spent the night at Claye [Claye-Souilly], where I was lodged in the White Horse.

On the 1st of April we dined at Meaux,[123] at the Siren, an establishment which is famous for its excellent hospitality, and we slept at Laferté [La Ferté sous Jouarre].[124] I lodged at the White Cross. The day had been very windy, with violent gales tiring the soldiers considerably. They were not yet accustomed to the fatigue of the march. On the 2nd of April, around Chateau Thierry,[125] the roads were terrible and there was a cold rain as we marched along. That evening there was a violent storm and a vast quantity of hailstones fell. On the 3rd we stayed where we were and I visited the town. It is divided into two by the River Marne. This is where Lafontaine was raised and you can still see the house in which he lived.

On the 4th, at Dormans,[126] we cut the day short and the weather was charming. But the soldiers were still tired. We had them do an hour of exercise when we reached the place we were to be billeted in. We also made them perform some exercises whenever we stopped en route for a meal. They were made to stand arms and break into sections and all because this would be the only training these troops would have before we encountered the enemy – we were obliged to instruct them as we marched along.

On the 5th, at Epernay,[127] I was lodged at the Cross of Gold but I went to dine with Captain Hilaire and his family. They are wonderful people and they welcomed me with all the warmth in the world. On the 6th and 7th, at Chalons [Chalons en Champagne], I stayed at the Imperial Palace.[128] I remarked that the mayors of the places we passed through always preferred to have us billeted in the local hotels and to have us dine there. That way we could be made to pay a great deal for our lodgings.

On the 8th of April we came to Auve, one of the poorest villages in France. So we had the troops billeted in the outlying environs. On the 9th we dined at Sainte Menehould [or Manheule] and ate a dish named after the town and which is very good.[129] We slept at Clermont [Clermont en Argonne] and I stayed at the Saint Nicolas Inn. On the 10th and 11th, at Verdun, I stayed with my former host, Monsieur Michel and, on the following day, dined with Monsieur de Marboeuf. On the 12th, at Mars La Tour, it was very hot and the dust was impossible. On the 13th, at Metz,[130] I was lodged at the Pheasant. We continued to exercise the troops. We also visited General Lorges, who commanded the military division, and the prefect.

We arrived at Courcelles [Courcelles Chaussy] on the 14th. It is a little village and troops were not usually billeted here. The Prince of Wagram dined at the inn I was staying in. On the 15th and 16th of April we were at Saint Avold and I stayed at the Carp.[131] That evening there was a great deal of thunder and lightning and there was torrential rain so the roads were all covered in water.

On the 16th the emperor dined at the staging inn. He spent 50 Napoleons on his dinner, and gave 100 Napoleons to the girl who served it to him.

My New Appointment
On the 17th, at Saarbrucken, I stayed in the Inn of the Three Doves.[132] On the 18th I was at Homburg, at the Post, and, on the 19th at Landstuhl, staying at the Dace. On the 20th and 21st we were in Kaiserslautern, at the Stag.[133] On the 22nd we were at Wenweiler [Winnweiler], staying at Number 115 with the deputy inspector of the forests. On the 23rd, we were at Alzey, at the Three Kings and on the 24th at Mayence at the White Horse.[134] On the 25th and 26th we were at Frankfurt and I lodged with Monsieur Bettman, the famous banker, and where I was very well received. There I learnt that I had been nominated as a colonel in the Guard.[135]

On the 27th, at Hanau, I was billeted at Number 473 on the square. On the 28th of April I left to join the 2nd Regiment of Tirailleurs of the Guard, the unit I had been promoted to command. I spent the night at Geinhausen, staying at Number 381 with a doctor who was prone to drink too much. I was well received and well treated. On the 29th I was at Schlüctern, at Number 4, the Trough Inn. The roads had been very bad.

On the 30th I was at Fulda, staying with the father of a colonel in French service. I dined at Madame Meige's, the niece of Monsieur Robertson, Councillor of State at Hanau. On the 1st of May I halted at Vacha and then I stayed at Eisenach at

Number 176. I visited my old lodgings at the Moorish Kings. On the 2nd I passed through Gotha and Erfurt, and lodged at Weimar, with Monsieur Müller, a councillor who lived at Number 43A. On the 3rd I passed through Naumburg and spent the night at Lützen. The town was full of wounded and prisoners of war, the houses had been sacked and I could not find anything to eat. The regiment was at Pegau, a pretty little town on the right bank of the Elster. The emperor of Russia and the King of Prussia had had their headquarters there on the day of the battle. The whole region is rather marshy and covered in woods so that it is most suitable terrain in which to wage guerrilla warfare. The area is fertile and rich in grain; there is also a great deal of fodder.

On the 4th of May I joined the regiment as it was camped close to Borna, a little town positioned on an island formed by the river. The roads were very tiring and bad.

On the 5th the division made a halt at Lausig [Bad Lausick], a little town almost totally constructed out of wood. We made camp just before we reached Golditz [Colditz], a pleasant town adorned with some attractive heights. The day had been long and exhausting. The road was not paved or melted and generally seemed to be slippery, with a surface which alternatively turned into either mud or fine dust. It rained throughout the night of the 5th to the 6th, something which rendered the roads impracticable. On the 6th the division camped to the left of Waldheim. The rain continued throughout the day. It was cold and generally very unpleasant. On the 7th of July the entire Young Guard halted in columns of brigade to the left of the road. The regiment was positioned close by the village of Nossen, with its right flank by the chateau. This village is situated on the left bank of the Mülda River. This river has its source in the Bohemian mountains, passes through Colditz and joins the Elbe near Dessau. The roads were getting worse and were so narrow that two wagons could hardly pass each other. In addition, they are interrupted by a vast number of bridges, all of which had been destroyed or burnt by the enemy.

On the 8th the division made camp on the left of the road, forming into three lines with our right on the village of Ober Corvitz [Gorbitz], opposite Dresden (which was less than a league away). This is where Frederick the Great had won his victory in 1745. From the heights around here, one gets a perfect view of the city and the course of the River Elbe as it meanders through an attractive and fertile plain.

Nobody could understand why the Emperor of Russia and the King of Prussia had selected such broken terrain in order to give battle, especially as the majority of their troops were cavalry and the French army had barely a single cavalryman to oppose them. The victory at Lützen was the consequence of this error, with the victory being entirely due to the French infantry. That infantry turned expectations on their head – it had previously been supposed that the French army, composed of untrained and inexperienced conscripts, would be beaten and destroyed. There was no doubt that had the field of battle been selected so that the Russian cavalry could deploy and manoeuvre, then we would have been lost. But the field chosen by the Russians was so broken that they became mixed up, confused and vulnerable to our artillery fire (which even managed to cause casualties by guessing where the enemy was). However, their retreat was carried out in such good order that they were ready to fight again just a few days later.

On the 9th it rained heavily, which turned our camp into something awful and unhealthy. We were using some old straw to fashion ourselves some rather poor shelters, structures which couldn't even keep the sun off us. On the 10th we entered the town just as all the convoys were distributing the rations (sometime between eight and nine o'clock in the evening). This meant that a lot of our equipment went missing. This is a real problem in the French army – there is an impatience which means that no delay in the execution of some action is tolerated at all, even though such a delay would not be dangerous. In such circumstances muskets, cartridge pouches, haversacks and equipment get lost. All this could have been avoided either by having us been ordered into the town before the distribution of rations took place or by deferring our entry until the following morning, and having us quit our camp then. It would not have made the slightest bit of difference to the military operations then in hand. It would not have had the slightest effect on us whether were billeted there at midnight or at eight the following morning, it was all the same as we were going to be lodged there for a number of days. But there is a kind of mania at work here, something which will be difficult to prevent as it comes from those who sit closest to the commander.

The emperor entered the town on the 8th of May whilst the enemy still held on to the new town on the right bank of the Elbe. The stone bridge had been demolished by the Russians. His Majesty lodged in the King of Saxony's palace which stands close by the bridge over the Elbe. The enemy had established some batteries on the other side of the river and did not cease to send over shot, shell and canister. This continued for a number of days and damaged much of the town and caused some casualties.

The regiment rested on the 11th, 12th and 13th. On the 14th it took part as the entire Guard received His Majesty the King of Saxony[136] close to the Gross-Garten palace on the road to Poland. The bridge which had been broken was now repaired and the entire army began to advance.

On the 15th of May, at around midnight, we suddenly received orders to prepare ourselves for battle. The entire unit remained in position until seven o'clock in the morning, believing that something might come to pass at any moment. We were at last ordered to march down the Dresden to Berlin road. The regiment made camp before Reichenberg. The battalions were placed in two lines between the two roads and one was behind the other with a distance of half a battalion separating them. On the 17th we set out at ten o'clock in the morning and continued forwards almost until nightfall. We camped near a large village whose name escapes me. On the 18th we performed some drill but heavy rain obliged us to stop. In any case, two minutes later, we were ordered to continue our advance. We followed the division and camped before Bischofswerda, a little town which had been burnt down. The division was positioned in two lines with a distance of a battalion between them. Two artillery pieces were placed to the fore and the rest of the artillery deployed between the town and our camp. The regiment was formed into a column of double companies and was positioned on the right between the two lines. That evening we learnt that a detachment of lancers had encountered a mass of Cossacks and had had a few men wounded by them. General Lanusse[137] was ordered to set out and reconnoitre the situation and he took the regiment with him at dawn on the 19th. As we marched along we were informed that the Cossacks had fallen back and were now around five leagues from where we then were. This determined the general to return to the camp. As we did so we found that the entire army had left and the men barely had time to eat some soup before we had to once more set out in order to rejoin the main body. We found the Young Guard before Bautzen, drawn up in three lines with the right resting on the village where the emperor was and the left close by the town. We faced the mountains of Bohemia.

On the 20th the battle of Bautzen began. The cannon fire began around nine o'clock in the morning and, around the same time, some lively musketry could be heard on the right. The division advanced and was directed towards the left of the town. The emperor had placed himself on a small height which dominated the entire plain. The Old Guard was drawn

135

up around this height, forming a kind of simple but very dense square. The Young Guard took up a position to the right of this height, and a little in front of it. We were formed in two parallel lines in closed columns of double companies with the battalions formed in a battalion mass keeping enough room to deploy between them. It then rained so violently that there was a pause in operations. When the downpour stopped, fighting broke out all along the line. Our left seized some heights upon which the enemy had maintained their camp. That action served as a signal for us to advance. Our units to the left of the town advanced towards some heights upon which the enemy had seemingly concentrated the bulk of his forces and from which we were separated by a deep ravine with sharply sloping sides. The banks of this ravine, through which flowed the twisting Spree, was littered with boulders. A bridge had been thrown hastily across the river, and the only crossing there was in this particular part of the field. The columns would have to cross one by one or make a great detour. As soon as we advanced the enemy pulled back some of his troops on the height to reveal a considerable battery of artillery. This battery, firing at close range, poured their fire on those troops who were now climbing the slope. These, despite the difficulties they found in negotiating their way uphill, nevertheless charged forwards and tried to deploy as soon as they could. There was confusion for a short time as the divisions, brigades and regiments became intermingled and order had to be imposed whilst under fire. This was achieved with comparative ease. The 2nd Battalion of the regiment was the first to gain the summit and formed up in closed columns. The 1st Battalion formed up to the right of the first. No sooner had the entire division been rallied than the brigade advanced, being directed towards a small hill on the left, which dominated the Spree. When we reached this position we formed a square with artillery positioned at each corner. It was then that General Lanusse fell, something which meant that he could not continue with the command. I was ordered to replace him for the rest of the day, which was largely spent manoeuvring until the enemy's second line was broken and the battle brought to a close.

Our casualties were light – we had two men killed and a few wounded. The army remained in position until the following morning. We were without fires, had no straw nor anything to eat apart from a small ration of very bad bread. The night was most uncomfortable.

On the 21st the battle of Wurschen was fought. This was one of the most important battles of the campaign, the results of which might just have brought peace had the emperor not so stubbornly insisted on standing by his unreasonable demands. As the troops took up their positions, the Young Guard had formed into two divisions under the command of generals Dumoustier[138] and Barrois.[139] The former commanded the Fusiliers and the Voltigeurs, whilst the latter had the Tirailleurs. The regiment formed part of the 1st Brigade under General Rottembourg.[140] No sooner had the division been organised than the brigade formed up into battalion columns. Some artillery fire began to be heard and the brigades were then formed into squares and began to march off like that towards a village whose name is unknown to me but which was probably just over a mile away from where we had first formed up. The bad road and the boggy nature of the ground meant that the squares began to break up and so we formed the men up in closed columns. Firing then broke out all along the line. The brigade took up a position alongside the artillery, then deployed amidst the rye, sheltered a little by an undulation in the ground just in front of them and in range of the redoubts the Russians had thrown up near the inn at Klein-Bascheville [Klein Bautzen]. It was from there that for six hours they kept up a hail of canister and shot against us, killing and wounding a number of men. We sent forwards some one hundred skirmishers to distract and worry the enemy gunners and we once again formed ourselves into squares. The emperor then sent up some 12-pounder guns and these were positioned to our right. We were then the targets of a sustained fire of shot and canister, the sky seemed to be on fire and the ground shook beneath our feet. I had never seen a struggle like this one, entire files of soldiers were blown apart and the number of wounded had risen to horrifying proportions. However, nobody quit the ranks to assist them to the rear, only those who had lost arms could move and go to find treatment, which they did without making the slightest complaint. The others, who could not walk, remained within the square without muttering a single word. Many of those who had been wounded in this way were killed by being hit a second time, dying in the arms of the doctors who were attending to their injuries. The plain to our rear was churned up by shot, and it was very difficult to attempt to cross it. A number of officers were killed attempting to bring us orders. We learnt that our left flank, which had attacked the Russian right, had been forced to retreat and had abandoned a redoubt which they had promptly seized. We thought that the battle was lost but it was at that moment that the emperor cried out 'Victory is ours'. Those who were within hearing distance thought that it was some kind of cruel joke, but, shortly afterwards, they perceived that his observation was indeed correct, and most timely. General Barrois then received the following order: 'The emperor orders the Barrois division to seize those enemy redoubts that are before it.' He had the first regiment formed up in closed columns of double companies and the second placed fifty paces behind in square. The salient angle of the first redoubt was given as the point against which we should advance. Some twenty-four guns were placed to our right and left and were to advance with us. A further fifty positioned at various different positions were brought to bear in support. We advanced forward at the charge but the enemy deemed it unwise to wait for us and abandoned the redoubts, leaving a few dismantled guns, a few wounded and a large number of dead to fall into our hands. The emperor had come up to the inn, had the division deployed and sent the regiment forwards to prevent the enemy establishing itself in a position over a mile from the inn. The skirmishers sent out before the column were enough to dislodge the enemy. I had my regiment deployed in two lines with a hedge to the left and some marshy ground to the right. I also had a few hussars with me and I had these placed to the rear, making do with an outpost placed before us to warn us of any enemy movements should they think that an opportunity might be there to attack us. The emperor came up to us and complimented me on the position the troops under my command had adopted. The night was brilliant and passed in perfect peace. The regiment had lost sixty-nine men on a day which had been one of the most glorious for the armies of France.

On the morning of the 22nd I received orders to rejoin the division, which had been sent off in the direction of Görlitz, where it seemed the enemy were in retreat. The regiment made camp in some woods close to Weisenfels. The vanguard exchanged fire with the enemy for some time but only a few roundshot reached us, causing us no harm. On the 23rd the regiment camped on a height between Reichenbach and Görlitz, quite close to the place where the Grand Marshal of the Palace, Duroc, was killed.[141] The two divisions of the Young Guard were reunited and were formed up in the following order: the first regiment drawn up in line, the second in square, the third regiment in line, the fourth in square and so on and so forth. Although we were on a height, the terrain in front of us was very flat and formed a very wide plain. The way in which the two divisions were placed seemed sensible to me as the enemy had a large body of cavalry quite close to where we were. The same formation had been successfully made use of at the battle of Lützen and, I believe, it was the first time it had been tried since then. The problem now was in how to place the police guard and how to have the men free to make their soup and lie down. This was how I solved the problem – I had the police guard placed in the centre of the square and shelters placed six paces behind the left and right of the square so that none of the sides of the square was inhibited. The kitchens were placed behind the 4th division of the 2nd Battalion. The companies kept six paces between them as when drawn up in column so that the 1st Battalion was to the right and the 2nd to the left.

On the 24th the division marched through Görlitz and camped just beyond the place. The town seemed quite substantial; it had quite a few pretty houses but the streets were generally very narrow and poorly surfaced. On the 25th the division was sent on to Valdau [Wykroty], with the regiment being detached to Bochdorf, a miserable village to the left of the road. On the 26th the Guard halted for a few hours close to Bunzlau [Bolesławiec] on the banks of the little Queis river so that the army could advance over some bridges. The regiment was then detached to Tomaswald, a poor village that had already suffered a great deal.

On the 27th the army arrived before Liegnitz [Legnica], the regional capital of Lower Silesia. Here I received medals for officers and knights of the Legion of Honour, accorded to the personnel of the regiment by his Majesty as a testament to his satisfaction on the conduct of the unit during the campaign. On the 28th we remained in the same camp. Talk of an armistice had begun and hope that a peace would be signed was everywhere. Liegnitz is quite a large city and the Prussians won a victory near here in 1760. On the 29th the two divisions of the Young Guard made camp behind Neumarckt at the junction of the roads from Dresden and Glogau [Glogow]. On the 30th the two divisions marched through the town and made camp on the other side, with the 1st Division to the right of the road and the 2nd on the left. The 1st Division formed up as two sides of a square so that the 1st Brigade would be able to deploy as needed. The 2nd Division formed a single line. Official news of the armistice reached us.

On the 31st of May orders were given out that the same kind of camp should be formed as had been established at Schoenbrunn and Finkenstein. Nobody appreciated what such a camp might cost; in fact it meant the ruination of the country for some fifteen miles around and the exhaustion of any supplies. It took us four days to complete our arrangements but it was of no use to us at all for we only stayed here until the 6th of June. Nevertheless it led to a great amount of pillage and the destruction of more than five hundred houses. On the 6th the regiment marched out at ten o'clock in the morning and spent a peaceful night at Parchwitz [Prochowice] and Attlais and in nearby villages. On the 7th, at Lueben [Lubin], quite a nice little town, ringed by town walls, I was billeted at Number 37 on the square. There were three young ladies there, all very friendly. On the 8th we arrived at Polkwitz [Polkowice] and were sent to our quarters. That of my regiment was to be around Glogau. There the principal villages are pretty much ten miles distant from one another and are: Quittitz [Kwielice], Bauch [Bucze], Rettkau [Retkow], Grambschutz [Grebocice], Porschutz [Proszyce], Tsohrewitz, Toppendorf [Potoczek], Wiesau [Radwanice], Pinquaurt, and Gross and Klein Obisch [Obiszow Wielki and Obiszowek]. It was in the latter that I established myself with my staff. The village is small, as its name suggests. There is a poor-looking chateau belonging to Prince August of Prussia, but this resembled a farm more than anything, and certainly not a palace belonging to a prince. The steward treated us quite badly. This is how we spent our days. In the morning, between seven and eight, we breakfasted, drinking a cup of coffee or chicory with a little milk, and at midday we dined with the master of the house, his sister and his children. Dinner usually consisted of some soup, some beef and potatoes and, for dessert, a slice of cheese. There were twelve of us at the table but we never had more than three bottles of wine or beer between us. We supped at eight in the evening, usually veal accompanied by a plate of vegetables and two bottles of wine. I never saw a man more phlegmatic than the steward. He carved the beef in a fashion which conveyed the utmost meticulousness, and it took time. So it was that, despite the paucity of the meal, we remained at the table for some two hours and it was frequently the case that the officers went without bread when the beef was served.

We made a number of trips to Glogau in order to buy necessities. Everything was so expensive and we were obliged to pay much more for these items than we would have had to in France. Silesia produces a great deal of rye, barley and oats as well as a great quantity of flax, from which the famous linen, so well known around Europe, is manufactured.

For a fortnight it seemed we would have peace, and I celebrated my imminent return to France where I would be able to recover my health following the Russian campaign. However, towards the end of the month of June, as hope diminished, I became convinced that this would not be the case. So, rather than imitating those colonels who hoped to present their regiments in the best possible light, and so bought them bright white breeches, I managed to obtain some grey trousers, which were roomy and comfortable, some black gaiters and sound shoes. My own feelings were confirmed when, on the 6th of July, we received orders to move to Polkwitz. I increased my efforts to have my soldiers properly equipped in order that they could be in the best possible condition. I had cases of scabies treated and, rather than sending my sick to hospitals, had them treated on the spot. When, on the 30th of July, the Duke of Treviso inspected us, my regiment had numbered two hundred more men than had been in the ranks at the time of the armistice.

142

Right after the review, the Duke of Treviso announced that the emperor's birthday would be celebrated on the 10th of August because it was possible that the armistice would end on the 15th and that measures simply had to be taken to concentrate the army. A notice was put up at the place where all the officers were to eat. The Duke of Treviso, our commander, presided over the dinner, which was very pleasant. There was only talk of how many victories we would win when the war recommenced, but it was easy to see through this boasting and perceive that the army had changed. And to predict the disasters that would come to pass.

The battle of Lützen, which we won against all the odds, should have persuaded the emperor to accept the peace that was being offered to him. It is difficult to believe that he was so ignorant of Germany that he could not be aware that all the German rulers were preparing to quit his ranks. How then would he be able to resist the whole of Europe? The enthusiasm that had inspired our battalions had been destroyed. Ambition had replaced duty, the army was commanded by men who were extremely brave, but they were inexperienced and poorly trained. The soldiers sought every occasion to absent themselves from the ranks, or to make their way to the hospitals and far from danger. It has to be added that they were beaten for the slightest of faults, that those who fell sick or could not continue marching were mistreated and abused, and it was simply not the case that they were being treated as companions in the struggle, or agents of our glory. Most of the officers and the generals were treating them as slaves, something which disgusted those who had nobler sentiments. Impossible things were demanded of them, things beyond the capabilities of man. And, in order to achieve those demands, the ends justified the means. The result was that if a man was even slightly ill, he would be more likely to die a miserable death than be treated and recover. This complete lack of humanity was the cause of us losing a vast number of brave soldiers. Observation would have shown how misguided this way of doing things was. It should have been clear that by forcing a few more men to stay with the colours they would have to fall out after a few days and then be lost forever. Treating them and allowing them to recover and rejoin the ranks at the end of the campaign would have been better. Well, indeed, this way of doing things, which is no more than good governance, was alien to the French army. Colonels and other officers who left men in the rear were criticised, rearguards consisting of NCOs and corporals were formed and they, by lashing out, forced exhausted men, who could barely stand upright, to keep marching. Those who were pitiless and without compassion were rewarded and flattered, to the extent that even those officers who were kind grew to be harsh and as barbarous as the others. The consequence of all this was that the soldiers no longer fought for glory, but out of fear. It was clear that a man who fell out of the ranks would put off trying to rejoin because he simply feared that he would be punished on his return.

I must now add one further observation, and that is that the administration of the army was so badly organised that at least three-quarters of the time the army had to do without meat. Captains were therefore obliged to send soldiers out into the countryside to pillage in order to avoid anyone starving to death. Soldiers abandoned in such a way are little more than ferocious beasts, capable of inflicting any manner of harm. There were examples to prove this from experience in Portugal, but this was ignored and nobody thought to takes measures to remedy the ill until it was far too late.

These observations meant that I was pessimistic, perhaps more than my comrades, but perhaps rightly, as events quickly began to show. I had predicted that we would be obliged to make forced marches and, given that Austria had declared against us, I was convinced that the emperor would be obliged to pull back to the Rhine and, at least for some time, wage a defensive war. All this despite his violent and excitable nature.

On the 11th of August the Russian and Prussian armies renounced the armistice. On the 15th we abandoned our camp at four o'clock in the morning and marched for the entire day along some really terrible roads. We camped near Scheinteiler, having marched seven German miles. On the 16th we continued our march, passing through Bunzlau, a little town on the heights above the Bobr. It is ringed with walls and a few redoubts had been thrown up. I was detached with the 1st Brigade and sent to Suberdorf, a substantial village in which the houses were spread quite far apart. The countryside was good, producing much grain, but the roads are terrible. On the 17th we arrived at Lauban [Luban]. I was detached with the first two regiments to Obersbertelsdorf [Uniegoszcz] on the road to Greiffenberg [Gryfów Śląski] and Zittau. The village was on the small side but the castle is vast, well maintained and the gardens are charming. I camped with one battalion behind a ravine, cutting the road, and with an outpost to the rear to keep communications with Lauban open. The rest of the troops were lodged in the barns and the castle.

We remained in the same position on the 18th and the battalion that had been encamped was relieved. I inspected the regiments, noting that the rest had been of great benefit to the soldiers who had been greatly fatigued by the long marches in recent days and, above all, by the rain and the bad roads. On the 19th we once again passed through Lauban and camped close by Luthnau [possibly Lichtenau, now called Zareba], a large and substantial village nine miles from Lauban. The valley between Lauban and Luthnau is charming and follows the path of a stream with immense fields to each side. It is in these fields that the flax is bleached in the sunshine, flax which is destined to be made into that superb linen for tablecloths which finds its way into all the great cities. I lodged in the mill along with Colonel Darieule [Darriule],[142] and we got on very well indeed.

On the 20th we marched out for a further nine miles in the same direction, the division halting in a plain and preparing its soup. We then received orders to march back to Lauban and we got back to that place at about midnight. It was raining, the rain was cold and it fell in torrents. They had us camp up on the hill above the town on the road to Lowenberg [Lwówek Śląski]. There wasn't a single stick for firewood, or a drop of water (apart from that which fell out of the sky and soaked us to the skin).

These marches and counter-marches at the commencement of a campaign have an effect on morale. It was not in the emperor's style to manoeuvre before giving battle. So we suspected that there was some uncertainty in these movements, and that there was perhaps an issue with the coordinating of our operations. The defection of Austria had been made known to the army and we knew that they had now joined ranks against us. This news made quite an impact on the reasonable ones amongst us, who now saw this as a prelude to our fall.

On the 21st the division arrived at Lowenberg, a little town on a plain and next to a river. It is ringed by heights, which create a kind of amphitheatre. Marshal MacDonald's corps had fought the enemy here the day before and had repulsed the enemy. Skirmishing continued on the higher ground. Those generals who were experienced in the art of war thought that the enemy had tricked us into attacking Lowenberg in order to draw us away from Dresden, divide our forces and defeat us in detail. We camped in the plain, formed up in closed columns and battalion masses. We were up to our knees in mud and water and I will never understand how it was we had been assigned to such an uncomfortable and unhealthy place. On the 22nd we stayed where we were whilst part of the Old Guard arrived, along with the 4th Division. We paid a visit to the generals. On the 23rd the army pulled back to Lauban for the third time, pausing briefly

146

just the once before camping close to the village of Lichtenberg [Bialogorze]. On the 24th the retreat continued, the regiment halting at Görlitz, where it received three days' ration of bread, and went to bivouac close to Kollwitz, only arriving there at close to ten o'clock that evening and spending the night in the mist and the horrible rain. The bad weather continued on the 25th, with hailstones now falling. They were so big and fat, and fell with such force, that a number of soldiers were wounded and the horses refused to go forwards. We camped in the woods of Bischofswerda.

Wounded

On the 26th the division arrived before Dresden. By now fewer than half the troops were present in the ranks; the strain had been so great that soldiers had collapsed into the ditches and were unable to continue. As you can imagine, it takes a tremendous amount of health and stamina to be able to endure such long marches and the fatigue our army had had to put up with. There are twenty-five German miles [1 German mile = 7.5 kilometres] between Lowenberg and Dresden, or 150 miles in all, and we did this in four days, in the rain and along horrendous roads. As we arrived on the heights above Dresden we could clearly see, on the far side of the city, that there were troops and artillery in position and that there was fighting. Just then a battery established itself on the left bank of the Elbe and opened up against some troops marching along the other bank. We rested for nearly ten hours, after which we were ordered into the city. The emperor was at the bridge, watching the regiments march past. We thought we were going into the city to be billeted and had no idea that we would be taking part in the fighting. But, as we drew closer to the Pirna Gate we distinctly heard the sound of musketry and shells and roundshot began to fall onto the houses close by. We came across the Grenadiers of the Old Guard in a little square and, a little further on, the Flanquers in

147

a kind of entrenchment. Next to them was a redoubt with a battery of six guns. These kept up a constant fire. This was the only place we held on the outside of the city. The enemy held Gross-Garten, a park which is within pistol shot of the Gate, and they kept up a tremendous fire against us, with their artillery also firing canister round after canister round. The Gate was within range of this and so it was that the regiment formed up under this murderous bombardment, and sallied out in columns at the charge. The first two platoons were sent out as skirmishers, the first battalion was directed at the corner of the woods and the second was sent directly against the enemy. The enemy was driven back at all points in a matter of minutes but nightfall meant that we could not profit from our success by pursuing the foe. The plain was covered with his dead, whilst I received two bullets and two fragments of canister in the chest and my two majors were also wounded. Monsieur D'Ethan [Dethan][143] would die from his wounds. The regiment also lost thirty-seven men killed or wounded. That night an icy rain fell and there was so much of it that the following morning we were up to our ankles in water.

The bad weather continued on the 27th. We formed up and skirmished with the enemy who now occupied the chateau in Gross-Garten. General Rottembourg having been promoted to general of division, command of his brigade fell to me. I had the 1st and 2nd Regiments of Tirailleurs under my orders. We were relieved by a division of Line infantry commanded by General Paillard.[144] I had met him before at Palencia in Spain.

The brigade was now sent against a village in which the enemy had established a battery of fifteen guns and which kept up an incessant fire against us. I had the soldiers formed up into closed columns and sent them forwards, making the most of the terrain and preventing the enemy from firing on us. The general sent me some twelve guns and I had these positioned to the left and right of the men, a little before our column. I advised the commander of the guns to concentrate his twelve pieces against a single enemy piece, destroy it and continue until not a single enemy gun remained in action. This method proved highly successful and by two o'clock in the afternoon, it was noted that the enemy fire had almost entirely ceased. However, the enemy replaced this battery with one of twenty guns of greater calibre, and this proved especially troublesome. The rain had continued in such force that the use of muskets was nearly impossible. The regiment had had thirty-six men wounded or killed, the wounded having been hit by canister. Most of these had to suffer amputation, and few survived. One of my servants was wounded. My valet was also hit as he was bringing me some bread and wine – he had his foot blown off by a shell. He had his lower leg amputated and recovered, but he was captured by some Cossacks as he was returning to France and I never found out what happened to him. That evening we were relieved by the corps of the Duke of Ragusa and we rejoined the Guard camped in the place where the Old Guard had been positioned during the battle.

On the 28th of August the regiment crossed through Gross-Garten and made camp at Zschawitz [Kleinzschachwitz] on the Pirna road. My wounds were starting to be really painful and they had only been cleaned using some salty water and covered with a single dressing. I therefore entered into a house in the suburbs of Dresden so that our surgeon could treat my wounds. The landlady was taken ill when she saw what a state they were in. But, in truth, I had been incredibly lucky. I had been hit by two pieces of canister shot just as I had reached the battery, one hitting me on the right, the other on the left. More than thirty others had passed through my tunic and torn my shirt into shreds. My tunic now had only four buttons, the other five having been carried off. My cravat had also been torn and my chest had so many bruises that it seemed completely black. And all this besides the two wounds on the right and the two on the left where I had been hit and the flesh broken.

149

After being treated, I rejoined the regiment that same day and continued to command the brigade. I found it very hard to make use of my left arm as one of the tendons had been damaged. I visited the chateau at Zschawitz, which belonged to a Russian prince.[145] The adornment on the outside and the interior decoration are quite unique and I have never seen anything like it before. It looked most comfortable and really quite handsome.

On the 29th we remained in our camp. On the 30th we were reviewed by the emperor in a field on the road which runs from Dresden to Berlin. I was still in the same state as I had been directly after the battle, with my torn tunic all covered in blood. This made an impression on the emperor, who kindly asked, 'Have you been wounded, colonel?' and closely examined those points where I had been hit. He made me a knight of the Order of the Iron Crown, and gave me the title of baron and an endowment which I never received but nor did I ever claim. He also rewarded me by granting the regiment a number of favours.

Annex I

Accounts of the Burning of Moscow by Personnel in the Fusiliers-Grenadiers

Corporal Jean Michaud in Moscow (1st Battalion, Fusiliers-Grenadiers)

Moscow, 24th of September 1812.

My dear father and mother, brothers and sister-in-law,

After having sent numerous letters to you without having received a response, I nevertheless hurry to send this one off so you can reply as soon as possible and keep me 'up to date' with your news, for I am kept in a state of unprecedented uncertainty from not having had word from you. I wrote to you from Hanau, near Mayence, and I certainly should have had a reply, and also from Vilna in Lithuania.

I don't know if it is a sign that you are unconcerned or whether the post is just not getting through, despite the fact that the postal service has always worked here, ever since we entered the country.[146] Perhaps my own letters have been lost en route because I can hardly believe that you would deliberately leave me worried and without word for as long as you have.

I can inform you that we arrived at Moscow on the 14th of this present month. We had a tough battle some thirty leagues from Moscow, but the Guard was not involved. Even so, the battle was very bloody and the Russians especially lost a lot of men. They had redoubts that were filled with corpses.

I can also tell you that Moscow has largely been burnt down for, two days after we entered the city, the inhabitants set fire with their own hands to the most beautiful houses in the city. We

151

found a number of large warehouses full of wine and flour, and other stores which were burnt down. The city has been given over to pillage since we entered but because it is such a large city you can always come across the odd house which has been spared. At the moment we are waiting to see whether it will be peace or whether the war will continue – at the moment it is uncertain which one it shall be.

I have found out what has happened to Vegrinot – he has been sick and has been travelling in his unit's baggage wagons. I haven't been able to see him. The regiment to which he belongs suffered heavily in the battle which took place on the 7th of this month. They lost two-thirds of their strength.

I don't know if we will march further or whether we will return to France. I am around a thousand leagues from you at present, so I hope we have gone far enough now.

There's nothing else to tell you at present, thanks be to God that I am perfectly well.

I close by embracing you with all my heart and I will always be your loving son. Please don't forget to send me news of my niece.

Michaud, Jean, grenadier in the Second Regiment, 1st Battalion, 4th Company of the Imperial Guard.[147]

Lieutenant Serraris in Moscow

14th of September: Universal enthusiasm. We saw Moscow from the summit of a hill, there it was with its 1,600 gilded domes, and we greeted it with cheering. We arrive in the city. We enter, with our bands playing.[148] We camp in one of the central squares. Patrols, shooting, disorder, pillage, and so on.[149] 15th of September: The fire begins. We believe it was started by accident. Ruin! We are detached in a sugar refinery outside Moscow – on the road to Siberia. 18th of September: An Armenian, with a turban and black beard, whose house we saved, welcomed me. I was of service to him. The large dagger he

152

carried was impressive. I stood guard at the university, a large and beautiful building which served as a sanctuary for all the French who lived in Moscow. 19th of September: We preserved our quarter of the city, to the right of the Kremlin, from the fire. 22nd of September: I am detached and posted at a mill at Svirlov, seven versts from Moscow. I was lodged in the palace of Monsieur Vysotsky. 23rd of September: The Cossacks and bands of armed peasants hereabouts start to vex me and begin to capture some of my men. I will play a trick on them. 26th of September: Every day I send a large quantity of flour to the city. Here there are around two thousand sacks of wheat to mill. 27th of September: Expedition, along with a detachment of Spaniards,[150] sent out to burn down a chateau at which some soldiers had been killed. 19th of October: We left Moscow, in the evening. We received orders to blow up the Kremlin.[151] 20th of October: We are to set out for Kaluga. The soldiers are weighed down with booty. We will rejoin the army two leagues from Moscow. We are harassed by the Russians, especially as we march through Moscow. There we capture General Wintzingerode and his aide de camp, Naritchkin.[152]

Sergeant Scheltens in Moscow
As we approached the capital the villages seemed to be more opulent and there were more of them. The columns of flames destroying them were also more common. At night our camps were lit up by these huge infernos. The soldiers were quickening their pace, despite the heat which good weather had brought back, when, all of a sudden, we reached the summit of a hill and found ourselves looking down on an immense city shining in a thousand colours and topped with resplendent golden domes. It was an incredible mix of woods, lakes, cottages, palaces, churches and belltowers. The soldiers cried out as one 'Moscow! Moscow!' That night the Guard camped in the Dragomelov suburb, close by the bridge of boats over the Moskwa River. The

next day, the 15th, we entered Moscow. Complete silence reigned, we were marching into a city of the dead. Huge flocks of black birds, crows and ravens, swarmed around the churches and palaces, lending the whole scene a most sinister aspect.

The army was divided up and sent into different districts of Moscow. Our regiment was sent towards Kaluga where most of the houses were still occupied by their French, Italian, German or Russian inhabitants. These had stayed, rather than following the Russian army as the rest of the populace had done.

How can one have believed that the second city of the empire would follow the fate of all the other towns we had passed through since Smolensk? The French army had hoped to find the shelter it had so long desired but, alas, that peace was to be of a very short duration.

The residents of the district we were billeted in brought us bread and ham but such luck was not to last. The day following the entry of the French, some flames could be seen rising from a large building which had been inhabited by ecclesiastics. We ran over but weren't surprised at this development, blaming the soldiers for starting the fire through carelessness. The fire was put out but, no sooner had this been done, than it broke out again in some other buildings. The bazaar, which was not so far from the Kremlin, was on fire. It was perhaps the richest warehouse in the world, full of Indian and Persian textiles. There goods from the colonies, tea, coffee, wine and spirits had been stored. The fire broke out suddenly and, a few moments later, everything had been consumed by the flames, despite crowds of soldiers trying to fight it. It proved impossible to stop the fire and so it was that pillaging began on a vast scale – it was a race to save such immense riches from the flames.

In such circumstances I managed to acquire a beautiful shawl from the Indies and a lady's fur pelisse. Plenty of things were broken or quickly swapped for something better.

The fire soon died down for lack of fuel. Carelessness was

still blamed. However, during the night of the 16th, the scene changed again – a strong autumnal wind got up and swept in from the east like a hurricane. It drove numerous fires westwards, towards the best parts of the city. In just a few hours, most of the houses and palaces were on fire. You could see huge tongues of fire stabbing out of the churches (there were 1,100 of them) and climbing up the belltowers.

It is impossible to conceive what this fire was like. You had to have seen it to understand the consternation that then gripped the army. Soon large numbers of wretches, which the government had left in the city in order to set fire to it, were arrested. They were interrogated and they were threatened. They soon revealed their terrible secret. Now there could be no more doubt. Military tribunals were established to judge the culprits on the spot and to shoot such arsonists or hang them. But the soldiers didn't go to the trouble of having them tried in this fashion, justice was more swift: a musket shot or a stab with the bayonet was an improvement on the slow deliberations of a court martial.

I still remember how our Lieutenant Serraris, a Belgian who eventually died in Dutch service whilst serving as a general at Maastricht, charged into the courtyard of a palace and thrust his sabre between the shoulder blades of one such wretch. The sabre broke and our Russian took a dozen more steps with the best part of a Guard's sword stuck in him. The others scattered in order to try to save their lives, but we brought them crashing down with our muskets. As for me, I came across one of them trying to light a fire in a drawer from a cabinet on the first floor of that very same palace. My man threw himself at my knees but I seized him by the throat, took him to the top of the staircase and sent him down, head first, all the way to the bottom. He wasn't killed by the fall, but a grenadier finished him off.

The wind got stronger and it was now a veritable storm made worse in the emptiness caused by the fire. It fanned the flames, pushing them here and there, and thus taking them to places where the arsonists had failed to reach. The flames were accompanied by terrible explosions and produced clouds of black smoke. These clouds climbed skywards but were then blown down towards the earth. The fire drew close to the Kremlin. The danger was real – there were four hundred caissons loaded with powder within the arsenal walls.

The emperor left the city, as well as the bulk of the army, leaving the Guard behind to watch over the Kremlin. Everyone was terrified by this horrible conflagration which lasted for the 16th, 17th and 18th of September. Then came the rain, following close on behind the strong winds. It started all of a sudden and the Kremlin was saved. Sentries had been placed on all those buildings which had been preserved from the flames and in which officers, wounded and sick were housed. The rest were left open to the curiosity and greed of the soldiery and they went in to seize food, spirits and clothes. The soldiers went into the ruins too, and penetrated right down as far as the cellars, finding provisions which were largely unharmed, or a little scorched. There was grain, meat, salted fish, wine, brandies, oil, sugar, coffee, tea, clothing, furs, silver, even Dijon mustard, all in abundance.

And there were a number of precious objects sold off at ridiculous prices. Other items were smashed, especially the finest porcelain and weapons of all kinds and from all countries. What was to be done with such things, two thousand miles from Paris! Sometimes we would come across buildings where the Russians had concentrated their wounded. These unfortunates had been unable to escape and had perished in the flames. It was calculated that thousands had died this way.

I was ordered to guard a Frenchman's house in the Kaluga suburb and had twelve men and two corporals under my command. The house was nicely furnished and only one part of the outhouses had been damaged by fire on the first day. My men went out marauding and brought back all kinds of foodstuffs, lots of wine and Champagne, a great deal of flour and sugar and, above all, excellent beer. They wanted for nothing, they even had mattresses to sleep on, true luxury for men who for years had come to appreciate the value of a good bed. The very day that we began guard duty at this house was the day that I performed an act of humanity towards a Russian. On the night of the 16th of September, when the city of Moscow seemed to be one enormous fire, I heard some cries of distress as I was running through the Kaluga suburb with my patrol. We headed over to where the noise was coming from and I was fortunate enough to rescue an old man from the clutches of some Polish soldiers who were dragging him along and threatening to kill him. After thanking me for what I had done, speaking French, which he did excellently, he then declared that he was Prince Gallitzin. His palace had been burnt to the ground and he appealed for my protection. I had him installed in a house opposite his palace, which belonged to a Frenchman, a professor of languages, and which was intact thanks to the efforts of my soldiers. The old man was well known in the house, everyone treated him with some deference and addressed him as prince.

The following day, Prince Gallitzin offered me 30,000 roubles to conduct him to the Russian lines or, if not, then to stay with him in his employment. As I was unable to accept either of these proposals, without harming my duty or my conscience, I suggested that the prince accompany me to headquarters and Marshal Bessières, commander of the Imperial Guard. He accepted on the spot. Prince Gallitzin remained in conversation with the marshal for quite some time. When he had finished I was sent back to the house with the prince and an escort of mounted Chasseurs. I would share what I had with him for the whole time that I was in Moscow, and this was to be his only resource.

I was rich in Moscow, I had gold. But what good was it to me?

I did find a kind of cloth which I thought was so much more valuable. It was laced, and embroidery in gold thread illustrated the twelve signs of the zodiac. They told me that it was used in the formal ceremony that went with the baptism of princes.

By the time I left Moscow my knapsack was pretty valuable. This was because one day, as I stood on duty at the Kremlin, a staff officer asked me if I knew what it was that was burning before my eyes. When I said I didn't, he told me that it was paper roubles. Most had been burnt, but I rescued perhaps two or three thousand francs worth.

During the time that the French army occupied Moscow, Napoleon, doubtless wishing to bring back some trophy to adorn Paris, had the enormous Orthodox cross brought down from the top of Saint Ivan's tower in the Kremlin. After lifting it free, ropes were then attached to lower it to the ground. It nearly hit the floor. This cross was left abandoned with the army's transport during the retreat. The gate into the Kremlin was sacred for the Russians and they always bowed and crossed themselves when passing through it.

Finally, on the morning of the 19th of October, after thirty-four days of rest, we left Moscow and marched towards Kaluga.

Annex II

Accounts of the Battle of Krasnoe by Personnel in the Fusiliers-Grenadiers

Lieutenant Serraris's journal entry on Krasnoe
17th of November: At Krasnoe. We face the Russians. At two o'clock in the morning, we advance against their camp, charge into it with fixed bayonets. We massacre them, that's the long and the short of it. Butchery. 18th of November: The second battle of Krasnoe, close by the ravine where our caissons became jammed. Not being able to save them, we paid the price under the roundshot and canister. The Russians sprayed us with canister. Our adjudant, Delaïtre, had both his legs blown off whilst he was aligning the line of markers. I replaced him, being immediately ordered to do so by the colonel. The 1st Regiment of Voltigeurs from our division was entirely sabred by cavalry. We pulled back, slowly, always subjected to the terrible canister, but in good order. Their roundshot struck our columns and inflicted casualties down their entire length. No wagons, no surgeons. Everyone who fell was lost and massacred in the rear by Cossacks. What a way of doing things! After two hours of marching the Russians left us alone. All our wounded perished. Not one remains.

In addition to Serraris's laconic journal, an account of the battle of Krasnoe was found among his papers:
Marshal Davout was pushing towards Krasnoe with his corps and the Russian generals Gallitzin and Barasdin were advancing against him. Ojarovski and Rosen were doing the same, and so it

was that the dancing began. The Young Guard, with Napoleon at its head, came and positioned itself between these last two Russian generals. The fighting was violent, but short-lived. Rosen made great efforts to break into Krasnoe, and push back the right flank of the Young Guard, but without success. Galitzin sent his cuirassiers into a charge against the 1st Regiment of Voltigeurs of the Guard, and also sent some infantry in support. At the third charge, the Voltigeurs were sabred with only around forty men and one officer surviving. The officer commanding the unit, Colonel Pion, was amongst those who were killed. At this stage of the battle, at around two o'clock in the morning, we left Krasnoe in order to go and surprise the Russians in their bivouacs. We marched maintaining the most complete silence, formed up in one square composed of all four regiments of the Young Guard. It was expressly forbidden to fire a single musket shot. So it was that we fell upon the Russians with the bayonet and they passed from a state of slumber into the arms of death. At dawn we took up a position just behind the Krasnoe road. The next day the battle recommenced. Our numbers were greatly diminished from the losses we had sustained the day before, and they would be reduced still further. The emperor, along with the Old Guard, had set off for Orsha, a pretty little town on the Dnieper and one where there was a bridgehead. This movement was of considerable urgency for without it, the Russians could have seized the position and the road to France would have been barred against us. At dawn we took up a position before the town and to the right of the main road which is called Catherine Strasse. As he was having us deploy on the left our sous-adjudant-major, Delaïtre had both his legs blown off just as he was aligning the line of markers. I was immediately ordered to take his place. The Russians were blowing wide and deep holes in the ranks of our division, but they were killing without defeating us. The soldiers stood waiting for death for more than three hours, without making any movement, without withdrawing one step. Roguet had lost most of his troops. It was now two o'clock and he nevertheless continued to astonish the Russians by maintaining a firm countenance. Finally the Russians, growing bolder, advanced and drew too close to the Young Guard. It could no longer maintain its position. Mortier therefore ordered the 3,000 men of the Young Guard still under arms to withdraw, step by step, before the fifty thousand Russians. 'Do you hear, my children,' shouted the general, 'the marshal orders us to march at the usual pace, at the usual pace, soldiers!' And this brave but unfortunate troop, dragging along a few of its wounded, and under a hail of shot and shell, began to slowly withdraw from the field of carnage as though leaving a parade ground.

Sergeant Scheltens on Krasnoe

On the 15th of November, the Russians took up positions at Krasnoe and, having cut our retreat, offered battle. On the 17th, Napoleon attacked them at the village of Ouvasovo [Uvarovo is meant], marching out at the head of the Old Guard. The village was seized, retaken and finally captured. Thanks, it must be said, to the Guard for it saved the debris of the army, at least for the moment. The retreat could now continue. There were so many bodies, and it was impossible to carry away the wounded so they all had to be left to die in the snows.

It was at this battle that I saw a regiment of the Young Guard, I think it was the 2nd Tirailleurs, which had been formed up into square, charged again and again, overrun and entirely destroyed. Not a man, not an officer, escaped.[153]

We lost a lot of men that day. Amongst them our Adjutant-Major, Delattre [sic], who had his thigh smashed by a roundshot. He asked me to pass him his pistols so he could kill himself, and gave me his gold watch. I still have it, heaven only knows what will become of it after I am gone. He was left on the battlefield and so it was that he was, like the other wounded, finished off by the Russians or by the cold. I have never been present, in all my time as a soldier, at such a murderous battle. The fighting was intense, roundshot was raining down and confusion was at its height. If we hadn't held on to Krasnoe until that evening, before being withdrawn towards Orsha, the entire army would have been captured. Over these few days the fighting cost the army, by which I mean the men still under arms, some 15,000 men as well as 7,000 stragglers. Of the 420,000 men who had entered Russia, just 24,000 combatants remained.

Sergeant Bourgogne on Krasnoe

Two hours after the Russians were encountered, the emperor and the first units of the Guard arrived at Krasnoe, including our regiment and that of the Fusiliers-Chasseurs. We camped behind the town but, upon my arrival, I was ordered to take fifteen men to provide a guard for General Roguet, who was then lodged in the town in some miserable thatched cottage. I established myself in a stable, happy to be spending the night under a roof and by the fire we had just lit. But it wasn't to be. Whilst we were at Krasnoe the Russian army, apparently some eighty thousand strong, was surrounding us so that there were now Russians before us, behind us and to our right and left, all of them no doubt sure they had us trapped. But the emperor would show them otherwise for, even if we were miserable, and dying of hunger and cold, there was still something which kept our spirits up – honour and courage. And so it was that the emperor, sick of being followed by that gang of barbarians and savages, resolved to rid himself of them.

On the evening of our arrival, General Roguet received orders to attack the enemy that night with a part of the Guard – the Fusiliers-Chasseurs, the Fusiliers-Grenadiers, the Voltigeurs and the Tirailleurs. At eleven o'clock detachments were sent out on reconnaissance to ascertain the enemy's position, thought to be occupying two villages, having made his camp in them, as could be seen by the light of their campfires. The Russians probably suspected we would attack because when we began to do so we found that some of them were already in position to receive us.

It was probably around one in the morning when the general came to me and said in his Gascon accent, 'Sergeant, leave a corporal and four soldiers here to protect my quarters and what little remains to me; you yourself return to the camp and rejoin your regiment with your men. We'll very soon have need of you.'

I will be honest – I was not happy to have received such instructions. I certainly was not worried about having to fight, but I regretted giving up on the rest that I had so much need of.

When I reached the camp everyone was already busy preparing their weapons. I found that they were resolved to fight, many telling me that they hoped that they would be able to put an end to their suffering, as it was impossible for them to go on.

It was two o'clock when the advance began. We set out in three columns: the Fusiliers-Grenadiers, where I was; the Fusiliers-Chasseurs with us in the centre; and the Tirailleurs and Voltigeurs on our right and left. It was as cold as it had been on the last few days and we marched with some difficulty with the snow up to our knees. After about half an hour we found ourselves amidst the Russians, some of whom were under arms for a large line of infantry had formed up on our right and was, at short range, firing into us with deadly effect. Their heavy cavalry, composed of cuirassiers in white tunics and black cuirasses, were on our left and were yelling like wolves to encourage themselves, without, however, daring to make a move. Their artillery, which was in the centre, was firing canister against us. This did not slow us down for, despite their fire and the number of men who fell from our ranks, we surged forward at the charge and burst into their camp, where we did frightful execution with our bayonets.

Those who were some distance away had had the time to rally in support of their comrades and so a different kind of battle commenced. They had set fire to the camp and to the two villages, so we could fight by the light of the fires. The columns on the left and right had outflanked us and were now entering the camp from the flanks, whilst our column took on the centre.

I forgot to mention that when the charge was sounded and when our column was driving back the Russians, and throwing their camp into turmoil, we came across hundreds of Russians whom we believed were dead or dangerously wounded. We marched through them, but no sooner had we gone past than they sprang to arms and opened fire. We were obliged to turn around to defend ourselves. Unfortunately for them, the battalion which formed the rearguard, and which they had neglected to notice, had arrived. They were caught between two fires and in less than five minutes they were wiped out. This is a trick which the Russians often use, but, on this occasion, it did not work.

One of the first of our men to be hit was poor Beloque, who, at Smolensk, had predicted his own death. He was struck in the head and died instantly. He was popular with everyone who knew him and despite the indifference being shown by all was greatly mourned by his comrades.

Once we had passed through the Russian camp, we attacked the village, forcing them to throw some of their artillery into a lake and pushing a large number of their infantry into seeking shelter in the houses, some of which were on fire. It was here that the slaughter was immense as we fought hand to hand. I found myself alongside our colonel, the oldest colonel in France, a man who had been through the Egyptian campaign. At that moment he was being supported by a sapper who held his arm; close by was Roustan the adjutant-major. We were at the entrance to a kind of farm and lots of Russians had been trapped inside by our men. There was just one means of escape open to them, an exit from the courtyard which was closed by a barrier which they would be forced to jump over if they wished to escape.

During the fighting I noticed a Russian officer mounted on a white horse who was lashing out with the flat of his sword against those of his men who were attempting to flee over the barrier and so had closed off their only avenue of escape. He was master of the exit but, just as he himself was preparing to leap the obstacle, his horse was hit by a bullet and went down, creating a further obstacle. The Russians were now forced to turn and defend themselves and, from that moment on, the fighting was terribly bitter. In the light of the flames butchery took place with Russians and Frenchmen, all intermingled, killing each other in the snow.

I wanted to get the Russian officer who had managed to crawl out from under his horse and who was, with the help of two soldiers, now trying to get over the barrier. But a Russian soldier stopped me from going further by pointing the barrel of his gun at me and opening fire. There was a flash in the pan but the musket misfired, just as well, because if it hadn't then that would have been the end of me. Although I felt that I was not wounded, I nevertheless staggered a few paces backwards whilst my opponent, thinking that I was badly injured, calmly reloaded. The adjutant-major, Roustan, who had been at the colonel's side, and who had seen me in danger, ran over and grabbed me, saying 'My poor Bourgogne, are you wounded?' 'No,' I replied. 'Well, don't let him get away.' Those were my feelings exactly. Thinking that my musket wouldn't fire (something which was very common because of the snow) I went at him with the bayonet. I hadn't given him enough time to reload but, even so, he was then hit and, despite being fatally wounded, he did not go down at once. He staggered backwards, glaring at me as he did so and not letting go of his weapon, and fell against the officer's horse that was blocking the barrier. The adjudant-major, passing close by, gave him a thrust of his sword in his flank, which hurried his demise. I then went back to be by the colonel and I found him worn out by fatigue and no longer capable of being in command. He only had his sapper to support him. The adjudant-major returned with his bloody sword and informed us that, in order to get back to us, he had had to fight his way through with his sword, receiving a bayonet thrust in his right thigh in return. Just then the colonel's sapper was hit by a bullet in his chest. The colonel turned and asked, 'Sapper, have you been hit?' 'Yes, my colonel,' said the sapper and, taking the colonel's hand, had him feel the hole the bullet had made. 'Here, my colonel.' 'You must leave the field.' The sapper replied by saying that he had enough strength to remain or to die here if necessary. The adjudant-major added, 'After all, where could he go, surrounded by enemies. We don't know where we are and it is clear that we'll have to fight on until daylight in order to try to find out.'

We were truly lost, blinded by the light from the fires. The regiment was now broken into detachments and was fighting all over the village. Scarcely five minutes had passed since the sapper had been hit when the Russians who we had trapped in the farm, and who now saw that they were likely to be burnt to death, offered to surrender. A wounded NCO managed to get through a hail of bullets to make the offer. So the adjudant-major sent me off to order a cease fire. 'Stop firing?' said one of our soldiers, who had been wounded. 'You can stop if you want but, as for me, wounded and likely to die, I won't stop until I am out of ammunition.'

He was indeed wounded as a shot had broken his leg and he was sitting in snow that was reddening with his blood. And he didn't stop firing; in fact he asked for more cartridges from his comrades. The adjudant-major, seeing that his orders were going unheeded, came over, saying the colonel had sent him. But our men, now fighting furiously, turned a deaf ear and carried on regardless. The Russians, seeing that they could not expect to be saved, and having probably run out of ammunition, were now starting to roast and so attempted to break out en masse from the buildings. Our men forced them back in. A few moments later, and unable to bear it any longer, they tried again, but no sooner had a few of them made it into the courtyard than the building collapsed, crushing the rest. Perhaps some forty perished in the flames, but those who had issued forth were scarcely any more fortunate.

After this episode we collected our wounded and gathered around the colonel with loaded muskets, there awaiting daybreak. As we did so we could hear firing all around us as the fighting continued at various points. Mixed in with these noises were the cries of the wounded and the moans of the dying. There is nothing sadder than a night action, where mistakes are often made.

We awaited the dawn and only once it had broken could we see the results of the fighting. The entire area around was covered with the dead and wounded. I recognised the man who had attempted to kill me. He wasn't yet dead, the ball had passed through his side and he had a wound from the adjudant-major's sword. I placed him slightly more comfortably, a little away from the officer's white horse because the animal could have done him some harm.

All the houses in the village where we were (I'm not sure if it was Kirkova or Malierva), as well as the Russian camp, were full of corpses, many of them partially devoured by the flames. Our major, Monsieur Gillet, had his thigh broken by a ball and died a few days later.[154] The Tirailleurs and Voltigeurs lost more than we did; in the morning I came across Captain Debonnez, who came from the same region as myself, and who commanded a company of Guard Voltigeurs. He had come over to see if I had come to any harm. He told me that he had lost a third of his company, as well as his second lieutenant (who was a Velite) and his sergeant-major (one of the first to be killed).

Following this bloody battle the Russians pulled back to a new position, which was not so far off, and we spent the whole of the 16th, and the night to the 17th, on the field of battle. But we did not rest, for every few moments they would call us to get under arms in order to keep us alert, so we couldn't rest or even warm ourselves.

Following one such alarm, just as we NCOs had collected and were chatting about our woes and about last night's battle, Adjudant-Major Delaître, the nastiest and cruellest man I have ever met, a man who sought to do harm for the fun of it, joined in our conversation and, something extraordinary, began by expressing his sorrow for the loss of Beloque. 'Poor Beloque!' he said, 'I'm sorry I ever did him any harm.' A voice, and I'm not sure where it came from, whispered loudly enough into my ear for others to hear it too, announcing 'He will soon die!' He seemed to regret the harm he had caused all those under his orders, and principally that done to us, the NCOs. There was not one man in the regiment who didn't wish to see him carried off by a bullet, and he was known as Pierre the Cruel.

On the 17th, shortly after dawn, we took up arms and, after forming up into divisional columns, marched off in order to take up positions by the road, on the other side of the battlefield. When we arrived we saw some of the Russian army established on some heights, with their flank resting on some woods. We quickly deployed into line opposite them. We had our left resting on a ravine which cut across the road which then ran behind us. This road was itself sunken and provided some measure of shelter and protection from enemy fire. On our right were the Fusiliers-Chasseurs, positioned about a musket shot from the town. In front of us, perhaps some 250 paces further forwards, was a regiment of the Young Guard, the 1st Voltigeurs, formed up into divisional columns and commanded by Colonel Luron. Even further forwards, a little over to our right and in the same formation, were the old Grenadiers and Chasseurs, as well as the rest of the Imperial Guard, including cavalry and infantry, who had not taken part in the fighting on the 15th and 16th. They were commanded by the emperor in person, and he had dismounted. Advancing with a firm step, as though at one of the great parades, he placed himself in the centre of the battlefield, opposite the enemy batteries.

After having taken up our position by the side of the road and opposite the enemy, I was walking along with two of my friends, Grangier and Leboude, following Adjudant-Major Delaître. The Russian artillery caught sight of us; it was well within range, and fired its first discharge at us. Adjudant-Major Delaître was the first to be hit. A roundshot cut off both his legs, hitting him just above the knee and above his riding boots. He went down without a scream, without even as much as a groan. He had been leading his horse by the bridle, carrying the reins around his right arm whilst marching along. As soon as he was hit we stopped because he fell in such a way as to be blocking our way forwards, and in order to go further on we would have to climb over him. As I was the one right behind him, I was the first to do this and, as I did so, I took a look at the man. He had his eyes open, but his teeth were convulsively chattering. He recognised me and called me by name. I drew closer to listen to him. He then spoke in quite a high-pitched voice to me and the others present, 'My friends, I implore you, take my pistols from the holster on the saddle and blow my brains out!' Nobody dared to do this service for him, nor would they for anyone else in a similar situation. Without replying, we stepped over him and continued on our way, which was just as well for, having gone around six steps further along, the second discharge from the same battery swept away three other men following along behind us, and also put an end to the adjudant-major.

Ever since the break of day we could see that the Russian army, which faced us on three sides (in front, on the right, and behind) was attempting to surround us. As it was doing so, and just after the adjutant-major had been killed, the emperor arrived and we prepared to let battle commence.

Each of the discharges from the enemy's artillery was terribly effective and killed many in our ranks. We only had a few pieces of artillery to fire back with but they, too, blasted holes in the enemy formations. However, some of our guns were soon knocked out. Throughout this time, our soldiers stood motionless, staying in this unhappy position until two in the afternoon.

Whilst the battle was being fought the Russians had sent part of their army to cut the road on the other side of Krasnoe and so prevent our retreat. But we stopped their progress by sending a battalion of the Old Guard against them.

Whilst we were standing exposed to the enemy fire, and having our numbers steadily reduced through casualties, we caught sight of the remains of Marshal Davout's corps behind us, and a little to the left. They were surrounded by a cloud of Cossacks who dared not charge them and who were dispersed by Davout's men as they drew nearer to us. When they were on the road behind us, I caught sight of a canteen man driving a cart containing his wife and children. The cart was hit by a roundshot destined for us, and, at that moment, we could hear the cries of distress uttered by the woman and the children, although we could not perceive whether anyone had been killed or wounded.

Just as the debris of Davout's corps filed past, the Dutch Grenadiers of the Guard [3rd Grenadiers] abandoned an important position and this was quickly occupied by Russian artillery which took aim against us. From that moment on, our position became untenable. A regiment, I have forgotten which one, was sent against them but it was forced to retreat. Another unit, the 1st Voltigeurs, positioned just in front of us, attempted to advance and got to the foot of the batteries but, just as it did so, a mass of cuirassiers (the same ones we had seen during the battle on the 15th, and who hadn't dared to charge us) appeared and forced them to withdraw. They fell back to the left of the batteries, and immediately in front of us, and formed into a square. No sooner had they done so than the Russian cavalry attempted to force their way in but they were met, at point-blank range, by a volley from the Voltigeurs and this brought a great many down. A second charge was attempted, with the same result and soon the ground by the sides of the square which the cuirassiers had attacked was covered with men and horses. However, the Russians succeeded at the third attempt, having brought up two artillery pieces loaded with canister which decimated the regiment. They broke into the square and began to continue the destruction with their sabres. Our unfortunate men, most of whom were young soldiers, many of them with frozen hands and feet, could not use their weapons to defend themselves, and were nearly all massacred.

This scene took place before us without us being able to do anything to help. Eleven men escaped; the rest were killed, wounded or taken prisoner, and these latter were driven off by blows of the sabre to a little wood over in front of us. The colonel himself, Colonel Luron,[155] was covered with wounds and was, with a number of officers, taken prisoner.

I forgot to mention that, when we were deploying ready for battle, the colonel had ordered 'Flags, and markers, take positions,' and I took up my post on the right of our regiment. However, nobody remembered to call us back in and, as it was one of my principles to remain at my post, whatever the circumstances, I remained where I was, with the butt of my musket in the air, for more than an hour, acting as some kind of motionless target for all the roundshot.

During this time, and just when the Russian artillery was

wreaking havoc in our ranks, the colonel was taken with a pressing call of nature. Neither our position nor the situation was convenient for such a function but, as he was desperate, he went off some sixty paces from the regiment, turned his back to the enemy, and calmly completed the deed. It was the cold which caused him most inconvenience; the Russians, who were aiming at him, barely troubled him, although he could see them quite clearly. It was as he was getting up from this position that he ordered 'Flags and markers, take positions.'

It was perhaps two in the afternoon. We had lost a third of our effectives, but the Fusiliers-Chasseurs had come off worse than us, being closer to the town and subject to more intense fire. About half an hour before, the emperor had set off with the leading regiments of the Guard and marched off down the main road. We were the only ones left on the battlefield, along with a few platoons from various units, and we faced more than fifty thousand enemy soldiers. It was now that Marshal Mortier ordered us to fall back and we did so, maintaining a slow pace much as though we were on parade, with the Russian artillery steadily destroying us with canister. As we pulled back we took with us those of our comrades who were the least badly injured. This was a terrible and sad ordeal, pulling back from the battlefield for, as soon as our poor wounded and those of the 1st Voltigeurs saw that we were abandoning them on the field of death, surrounded by enemies, a few tried to drag themselves along, reddening the snow with their wounds. They raised their hands heavenwards, screaming out for our help. But what could we do? The very same fate awaited us at any moment and so it was that in our retreat we were obliged to abandon anyone who fell from the ranks.

We passed the position which was to our right and had been occupied by the Fusiliers-Chasseurs. They were now marching in front of us, and as our second battalion, in which I served, was acting as a rearguard, I saw a great number of my friends stretched out on the snow or horribly mutilated by canister. One of these was a young NCO with whom I got on well. He was called Capon and was from Bapaume, from a region close by my own.

Once we had passed the position occupied by the Fusiliers-Chasseurs we drew closer to the town and saw, on our left, about ten paces from the road and by the first house, some artillery pieces doing their best to support us by firing on the advancing Russians. They were supported by around forty men, partly Voltigeurs, partly artillerymen, all that remained of a brigade commanded by General Longchamps.[156] He had once been in the Imperial Guard and he was there with whatever remained to him, to save them or die with them. No sooner did he notice our colonel than he came over to embrace him. They hugged like two men who had not seen each other for some time and who were, perhaps, meeting for the last time. The general, his eyes brimming with tears, spoke to the colonel whilst showing him the two cannon and the handful of men he had. 'Look, that's all I have!' They had been through the Egyptian campaign together.

General Kutuzov, who commanded the Russians during the battle, is supposed to have stated that the French, far from allowing themselves to be crushed by the extremity of their circumstances, rushed all the more furiously against the Russian guns that were destroying them. General Wilson, the English general who was present at the battle, called it a battle of heroes. This certainly wasn't because he himself was there, for that's a word which can only be applied to men like us who, a handful of men, fought against an army ninety thousand strong.

General Longchamps and his men were soon forced to abandon his guns as most of his horses had been killed. He followed on behind us and we made the most of the terrain during our retreat to protect ourselves as we withdrew.

We had scarcely begun to enter Krasnoe when the Russians, who had mounted some artillery pieces on sledges, arrived at the first houses and fired canister into them.[157] Three men from our company were hit. A shell struck my musket, split the wood and bruised my shoulder, and then went on to knock the head off a young drummer marching in front of me, killing him instantly.

Krasnoe is split into two by a ravine. When we approached it we saw at the foot of the ravine a herd of cattle that had died from cold and hunger. They were so rigidly hard from the cold that our sappers could barely cut bits off them with their axes. Only their heads were showing and their eyes were open as though they were still alive. The livestock had been intended for the army but had not been able to reach us, as want and hunger had killed them off.

All the houses of this miserable town, along with a rather large monastery, were full of wounded men who, when they saw that we would abandon them to the Russians, began to scream. We were obliged to leave them to an enemy who was savage and pitiless, who would plunder these unfortunates without regard to their rank or the seriousness of their wounds.

The Russians were still following us, but warily. A few guns still fired on the left of the road, but they were not very effective. The road we were marching along was sunken and so the Russian shot passed overhead and couldn't hit us and the presence of what remained of our cavalry kept them from getting any closer.

By the time we were a few miles from the town we were a little safer. But we were marching along in silent sadness, thinking about our situation and the unfortunate comrades we had been forced to abandon. I could still see them, begging us for help. Looking back we could see some of our lightly wounded who were stripped from having been plundered by the Russians who then left them where they were. We were lucky enough to have these ones saved, at least for the moment, and we hastened to give them what we could, and to cover them up.

That evening the emperor slept at Liadoui,[158] a village built out of wood. Our regiment established its camp a little further on. As I was passing through the village where the emperor was, I stopped to warm myself by a fire by a miserable hut. I had the good fortune to discover Sergeant Guignard, who was from my region, along with his Hungarian cantinière. I partook of some broth and some horsemeat with them, and this made me feel better. I really needed it because I felt so weak, not having eaten anything for two weeks. He told me that, during the battle, their regiment had suffered a great deal and they were much reduced in number. But that was nothing compared to us, because he knew how many we had lost during the night of the 15th to the 16th and in the fatal day that had just passed. He added that he had thought of me a great deal, and he was glad to see me now, all in one piece. He asked for news about Captain Debonnez, but I couldn't tell him anything, not having seen him since the morning of the 16th. I left him in order to rejoin the regiment, which had established itself close by the road. The night was terrible; it snowed heavily and this soaked us through, and there was also the cold wind, and the lack of fire. Still, it was nothing compared with what was to follow.

Notes

1. A view shared by General Roguet: 'The division was, in point of fact, the best in the army. The officers had prospects and the soldiers, the oldest of whom was barely thirty, had already experienced the difficult campaigns in the Peninsula. Their appearance, administration and discipline left nothing to be desired.' He also lavished praise on the division's superior officers: 'The generals and superior officers of this division were young, robust, energetic, experienced, and military men in the true meaning of the term.' Scheltens thought 'we were young men at our peak, well-trained, always jolly and full of song, and commanded by experienced officers who had come from the Guard'.
2. Something not unusual. General Roguet had 'a coach, two wagons, books, lots of maps, twelve horses, six servants, and the other officers were likewise equipped'. This was just as well for Vionnet because Scheltens, in the ranks, noted that 'we spent five or six days without bread before crossing the Niemen on the 24th'.
3. Serraris crossed on the 28th of June, noting that 'we crossed the Niemen three-quarters of a league from Kovno, and we were within sight of this place'.
4. The regiment was inspected at Vilna on the 8th of July. General Roguet described the event: 'The chief of my staff, Lebeau, notified the emperor, who was at Vilna, that the Fusiliers-Grenadiers were approaching. "Have them eat," said Napoleon, "and indicate to Roguet that he should halt at the entrenched camp. I wish to review his troops." Soon after the last battalion had marched in, the emperor arrived.

He asked me how many effectives I had, seemed astonished at the speed of our march and that, despite the length of the march, we had only left sixty-three men behind. He was in a good mood, spoke to many of the officers and told the soldiers a number of times "What brilliant youth! They are pretending to be tired because they have come all the way from Salamanca. My Old Guard will be jealous of them – treat them well."'

5. It had been a busy time. Two Fusiliers (Erasme Ernout and Jean Bricteux) from Belgium sent this note back to their parents on the 3rd of July: 'I can't really write much to you as we don't have much time. I only have two minutes to write you this.'

6. Lieutenant Serraris had noted that the countryside in Poland had been stripped bare: 'The countryside has been devastated by the passage of troops,' he wrote on the 12th of June.

7. The sentiment was echoed by Serraris: '17th of July: entered Glubkoe, a little wooden town. Only Jews are to be found here.'

8. Marshal Joachim Murat (1767–1815), son of an innkeeper but elevated to kingship in 1808. He commanded the Reserve Cavalry, and frequently took charge of the French vanguard.

9. Vitepsk was where Serraris came across two Flemish hostel keepers and 'it was here that we brewed beer which came back to haunt me'. He was sick for some days. Bourgogne was more fortunate; he enjoyed the beer, and saw that the rest of it went to the cantinière and was then sold to men of the unit.

10. A sentiment echoed by François-Joseph Detiège, a Fusilier, who sent the following from Vitepsk on the 4th of August: 'We are in Russia, pursuing the Russians. We are six hundred and fifty leagues from Paris and we are still

marching further away. It is a poor place to be marching through, especially when the weather is bad, as it is a difficult country. I have to say that we are not doing very well in terms of food. Fortunately, just at the moment, we are amongst the peasantry. We had some good times along the way, especially in Silesia, where we were billeted amongst the peasants. But as soon as the emperor arrived, we began marching for great distances.'

11. Baron Fain said of Vitepsk: 'This town of Vitepsk, from where I am writing to you, is another one stuffed with Jews. Once you have seen one Polish Jew, you have seen ten thousand.'

12. Deblais, no longer in the Fusiliers, noted that 'there is a big parade in front of the palace every day, and some houses have been knocked down to enlarge the parade ground; we are there every day in full dress.'

13. Scheltens saw the wounded from that battle having their wounds bandaged using papers from the state archives of Smolensk. 'All the dead', wrote Scheltens, 'were rendered hideous and pestilential under the burning sun.'

14. The emperor, riding his horse Lutzelberg, spent twelve hours exploring the battlefield, returning to his headquarters in a coach at four that evening.

15. Marshal Louis Nicolas Davout (1770–1823) had reorganised the Polish army after 1807 and was, perhaps unfairly, accused of having regal ambitions, although Prince Poniatowski was a more likely candidate for the Polish throne.

16. The Ancient Greek name for the Dnieper River, which flows from the Valdai Hills to the Black Sea.

17. A verst is a unit of measurement which is just over a kilometre or two-thirds of a mile.

18. General Mikhail Kutuzov (1745–1813) was a veteran of the wars against the Turks. He had been wounded in the

temple, and lost the use of his right eye, in 1773. In 1811 he had again fought the Turks, but was appointed to lead the Russian armies in the defence of Moscow on the 20th of August 1812.

19. It was at this point, with General Sorbier's Guard artillery raking the Russian position, that a decisive blow was expected from Napoleon – namely, that he would launch the Guard against the Russian lines. Roguet, with his division drawn up behind Friant's division, reports that Murat sent General Belliard to request such a move, but Napoleon declined, saying: 'Nothing is clear to me; if there is a second battle tomorrow, what shall I fight with?'

20. Serraris restricts his account of the battle to the following: '5th, 6th and 7th of September – Battle of La Moskova; it was hot work.'

21. The peace was signed at Tilsit between the French and Russian empires on the 7th of July 1807. The two emperors met on a raft on the Niemen and then reviewed the French and Russian armies.

22. Serraris noted 'Mojaisk was taken. We form the vanguard under Mortier and are twenty-five leagues from Moscow.'

23. Baron Fain mentions that the army camped through its first frost of the campaign that night.

24. Serraris is growing weary of the slow progress, as his journal entry for the 10th to the 13th September reads: 'Action in the vanguard. It never ends and is starting to bore me.'

25. Marshal Edouard Mortier, Duke of Treviso (1768–1835), was nominated governor of the city by Napoleon. Roguet remembered that 'The Duke of Treviso was appointed governor – the choice could not have been better. My division entered the city first.'

26. Constructed in 1792 and now again called Tverskaya Square, this was known as Soviet Square when Moscow was

the capital of the Soviet Union. The Governor's residence was at number 13. Bourgogne confirms that 'We arrived at the Government Square, where we formed up opposite Rostopchin's palace; he was the governor, the one who would burn the city down.'

27. A valuable commodity, it was already selling at 12 Francs a bottle, according to Fain, which was one month's pay for a line infantry drummer. Deblais, now serving in the Old Guard, wrote that wine cost 8 Francs when he first entered Vilna, but it soon went up to 12 or 15 and was 'probably tampered with'.

28. This might seem strange as Sergeant Bourgogne wrote that, 'We were told the whole regiment was on picket duty, and that nobody should, under any pretext, be absent from the unit. However, an hour later, the square was covered with everything that you might ever want – wines of all kinds, liqueurs, preserved fruit, and a prodigious amount of sugar, some flour, but no bread. They had begun by going into those houses on the square and asking for food and drink but, finding nobody was there, they helped themselves.'

29. In January 1811 some 130 conscripts from Tuscany and Rome were drafted into the regiment, along with 333 Dutchmen. These regions had been absorbed into the French empire.

30. Marshal Edouard Mortier, Duke of Treviso (1768–1835).

31. General Roguet, commanding Vionnet's division, wrote that 'The Russians set fire to the Stock Exchange, the Bazaar and the Hospital but we, at first, managed to contain the fire. The enemy had left behind some ten thousand criminals so they could burn down the city.'

32. Roguet says that he left for the Petrovskoe Palace, and came back the following day. Bourgogne says he left the 2nd Chasseurs on duty, but took the rest of the Guard with him, fearing the Guard's artillery wagons would explode.

Napoleon had left on the evening of the 16th, but was back in the Kremlin on the 18th (a Friday).

33. Marshal Mortier sent word to Berthier on the 18th of September that the area around the Marshals' Bridge had burnt but the surrounding neighbourhood had been saved and that 'the 5th Company of the 2nd Battalion of Miners under Captain Tholosé, and the Fusiliers of the Guard, have shown considerable zeal'.

34. General Roguet states that 'three hundred of these incendiaries were taken and shot'. Colonel Pierre Bodelin, Vionnet's superior, was on the commission. Bourgogne seems to have misunderstood as he says that orders were given to shoot anyone found setting fire to buildings, rather than arrest them.

35. Corporal Michaud wrote that 'The city began to be pillaged as soon as we arrived but, as it is a very large city, there are still some warehouses which are still untouched.'

36. Vionnet probably means Youri Neledinski-Meletzki (1752–1829). He had studied in France, and fought the Turks in the 1770s, obtaining the rank of colonel under Czar Paul I. He had retired in 1809 to write poetry.

37. Roguet, the arch disciplinarian, lamented 'Meat was distributed but the disorder grew worse; the pillagers, chiefly from the administration or foreigners, discovered the cellars and stores which had survived the fire. They laid waste to them and completed the destruction the Russians had begun.' Bourgogne was clear that 'once they knew that the Russians themselves had torched the city, it was impossible to restrain the soldiers; everyone took what he thought was necessary, or even things for which he had no use'. His own captain had him take ten men to go out and look for food. Orders directed against pillaging were issued on the 20th, the 21st and again on the 29th.

38. General Roguet noted that 'two hundred out of the four

thousand stone houses, five hundred of the eight thousand wooden houses remained. Some eight hundred and fifty churches were more or less ruined.'

39. This is an exaggeration – the population in 1812 was closer to 250,000 inhabitants.

40. The mortar and culverins were cast by Andrey Chokov. The mortar was produced in 1586.

41. The great victory over Charles XII of Sweden in 1709, when Peter the Great trounced the Swedes, who had wintered in Minsk before advancing into the Ukraine; most of the Swedish army was captured, although Charles himself escaped into the Ottoman empire.

42. A distribution of brandy was made each day, but only to men of the Guard, from the 23rd of September 1812.

43. Vionnet did well. Baron Fain bought such a coat for 200 Francs, a Line infantry captain's monthly wage. Roguet did even better. In Spain in 1811 Godet had given him a useful gift: 'As a mark of respect and gratitude to General Roguet, I left him a magnificent fur coat made from bear skin which had served me well in a number of bivouacs.'

44. Roguet says that Lauriston was sent to Kutuzov's camp with terms on the 4th of October, although his dates are often wrong.

45. Roguet states that '4,000 irregulars, transformed into Cossacks by the landowners, surprised a division of light cavalry, took two batteries and caused 1,000 casualties'. Napoleon had noted on the 29th of September that 'the number and audacity of bands of armed militias is on the increase. A convoy of pontoons and pontonniers under Captain Michel was captured at Gjatsk on the 15th.'

46. Monsieur Bausset, prefect of the palace, had been tasked to organise such distractions. From the 21st of September onwards, Madame Bursay gathered a troupe of actors and actresses from amongst the expatriate French community in

Moscow. They put on the play *The Jeu de l'amour et du Hasard*, amongst others. One of the actresses (Liselotte) would travel back from Moscow with Marshal Mortier but was captured at Vilna; another (Louise Fusil) left a dramatic account of the retreat.

47. Bourgogne tells a long story about looking after two Russian women who served as laundresses for the company, and who perhaps provided other services.

48. Count Nicholas Petrovitch Cheremetiev (1751–1809).

49. This palace was to be used by the Dragoons of the Guard as a billet.

50. Lublino, or Lyublino, was sold in 1800 to Nikolai Durasov, who largely rebuilt it.

51. Petrovsky, named after a previous owner, Czar Peter the Great, had passed to the Razumovskys in 1766. Count Alexey Razumovsky lived there whilst his brother, Gregor, owned the extensive grounds at Gorenki.

52. Vionnet uses the classical term the Straits of Zabache, better known as the Bosphorus, but the Black Sea is meant.

53. Roguet was of the opinion that 'the Russian peasant is better housed, fed and dressed than the Poles, especially those in the Duchy of Warsaw'.

54. Scheltens was told by an officer that the paper money was forged, adding insult to injury.

55. This is an accurate approximation, the paper rouble was worth 0.25 of a silver rouble.

56. Roguet wrote that he had 3,600 infantry with him, as well as four hundred men of the 12th (Polish) Lancers and 1,200 dismounted cavalrymen, and that the emperor 'had ordered him to escort the treasure and the intendance headquarters. I had with me all the trophies carried off from the Kremlin.'

57. It was hard work, as a letter from Roguet to Marshal Berthier noted: 'The wagons loaded with the Moscow

trophies can't move any further. I have to let them rest at Gorki and I have left a battalion there to guard them. The major in command of the battalion has orders to march at four o'clock in the morning precisely. I have also charged him with escorting the 20th Train Battalion with wagons loaded with flour for the Guard.'

58. This was where IV Corps encountered and defeated the Russians, but the battle was costly and reduced Napoleon's effectives still further.

59. The army found a quantity of onions here, much to the relief of the soldiery.

60. Bourgogne, who was on sentry duty close to the imperial household, heard the same cries, ran across the ravine and saw the results of the fighting. He thinks the mounted Grenadiers had charged to save the emperor.

61. Serraris mistakenly has this happening on the 21st of October. He also notes that the unit was formed up into squares and sent out on reconnaissance in that formation.

62. Serraris noted that 'None of the dead from the action on the 9th [Borodino] had been buried. All the French wounded had been collected and were on either side of the road. They were placed even in the emperor's own vehicles.' Bourgogne remembered a miserable night, 'camped close to the Great Redoubt where General Caulaincourt had been killed and buried'. The troops used broken muskets to keep their fires going.

63. It was at one of these fires that Bourgogne spoke to a Portuguese captain charged with escorting eight hundred Russian prisoners of war. These weren't being fed, and were reduced to eating each other, according to the escort.

64. Nicknamed the city of schnapps by the troops, it was here that Napoleon sent Narbonne to ask Roguet about his coach and why it hadn't been burnt. When Napoleon 'learnt that it was mine, he did not say anything and when an artillery

general insisted, he first pretended not to hear him, and then said "Leave it alone, if it can move."' Scheltens thought that the baggage train was still excessive: 'Each company had a few carts containing provisions amassed from amongst the ruins of Moscow. Added to this was the booty from all those abandoned warehouses.'

65. Bourgogne and the NCOs, overseen by Roustan, were to march at the rear of the column and prevent the Fusiliers from staying behind to warm themselves at camp fires.

66. Bourgogne described it as 'a blockhouse, or military establishment, a kind of big, fortified barracks, occupied by soldiers of different regiments, and the wounded'. Those fit enough then accompanied the army, the rest were left behind with some surgeons. The church where the emperor slept and the blockhouse were at Semlevo.

67. It was here, at Jaskovo, that many of the Moscow trophies were abandoned, along with some guns.

68. The city of cabbages, according to Bourgogne, but only because of the cabbages the army had found on the way to Moscow. The regiment camped at eleven o'clock that evening, finding enough firewood in the half-burnt town. The following morning, portable flour mills were issued to the regiment.

69. The cantinière, Dubois, gave birth that day but the baby died shortly afterwards.

70. At Mikalevska, where Napoleon first heard that General Claude de Malet had been conspiring against him in Paris.

71. This was at Mikhailovka. Roguet saw this wine being sold off by the imperial servants in Smolensk a few days later. They were charging 20 Francs a bottle, and there was a crowd at the entrance to the cellar where it was being sold off.

72. He did better than Bourgogne, who paid 15 Francs for seven potatoes; he secretly ate one so his comrades did not realise, only to find the rest frozen the following morning.

73. The vehicles were stuck in a ravine, according to Bourgogne, who saw that the horses were unable to pull the guns of the Guard Artillery uphill and out of this obstacle. The Fusiliers spent the night to the right of the road, next to some Prussian gunners, whilst Bourgogne was on sentry duty, guarding Marshal Mortier, Colonel Bodelin and Roustan.

74. Serraris arrived on the 10th of November: 'Arrived at Smolensk at two o'clock in the morning. They offered me some bread, some brandy, some mutton and a warm room. I slept there, on the straw. I felt myself transported to paradise and forgot all my toil and suffering.' Scheltens had arrived on the 9th, 'my comrades and I were hopeful of finding food. The stores were soon pillaged and we could only get hold of some flour the whole time we were there.' Some Guard units were, however, issued rations.

75. A province of the Ukraine to the northwest of Kyiv, taken from Poland during the partitions in 1793 and 1795.

76. Bourgogne noted that 'one hour after we arrived, we were issued with a little flour and an ounce of biscuit'. Sergeant Grangier and some men of the regiment who had gone on ahead with Marshal Bessière's wagon, and who had arrived a few days before Bourgogne, were more fortunate and had helped themselves to some of the city stores. Bourgogne found nineteen men of the regiment in a church.

77. At Korouitnia, according to Colonel Meynadier on Mortier's staff. The Fusiliers were in the vanguard.

78. Roguet had sent out Captain Lucotte to steady the other regiments, but they were swept away and he then relied on the Fusiliers-Grenadiers to cover their retreat. Roguet says that there were forty-one officers and 761 other ranks killed that day, with 1,500 men falling into enemy hands.

79. At Liady.

80. This seems wrong – Dobrouna was reached first, with

Napoleon narrowly escaping a Cossack raid, then Orsha, where Napoleon encountered the musicians of the Guard and had them play the Chant du Depart. The army's pontoons were burnt here, forcing the improvisation of bridges a few days later, and Roguet lost his correspondence and journal.

81. Bourgogne remembered it as 'a village of which only a barn, which was serving as the post house, and two or three houses remained'.

82. This was II Corps, which had been to the north of the line of the retreat, and was attempting to hold the Russians under Wittgenstein at bay.

83. Russian divisions had been stationed in Moldavia following a campaign against the Turks in 1811. Peace was signed between the Ottomans and Russia in May 1812, and the Russian troops marched northwards.

84. One bridge was intended for vehicles and artillery, the other for those moving on foot.

85. The Fusiliers remained behind long enough for Bourgogne to go off and find some flour and then, with one of the regiment's musicians, cook some pancakes. The regiment crossed later that night and Bourgogne, despite his fever, was sent back to the bridgehead to collect stragglers. He found five Fusiliers and the regimental armourer.

86. Serraris does not seem to have been with the rest of the unit. He related, 'The bridges are blocked. Confusion, despair, cursing, swearing. I made a passage through to the bridge using my sword.'

87. Victor's IX Corps protected the crossing; it included a Polish division but also a number of Hessians and troops from Baden.

88. Bourgogne, now with seventeen stragglers from the regiment and the blind Sergeant Rossière, was still by the bridge, but was soon reunited with the regiment. The good

sergeant then fell asleep, only to be woken by Lieutenant Julien François Favin pulling his ears to keep him awake.

89. It was here, notes Roguet, that the rest of the Moscow trophies were abandoned and dumped in the marsh. Bourgogne noted that 'we crossed over pine bridges a thousand paces long which the Russians had not, thankfully, had the opportunity to burn'.

90. There were some potatoes earlier; Villeminot, a cuirassier officer, noted in his journal that on the 30th of November 'we began to find more and more potatoes'. This was borne out by Bourgogne, who found three 'slightly bigger than a nut' just before he reached the village.

91. It was here, a village christened Miserovo, that Bourgogne and Leboude [actually Jean-François-Nicolas Leboutte] of the regiment drank some bad gin, fell in a ditch and were rescued by some Westphalians. The next day Bourgogne lost the regiment, and only caught up again after Smorgoni. The men asked him whether he had found any food, and on his negative reply, 'swore and beat their musket butts on the ground'. This Leboutte (given as Leboude by Bourgogne, or Leboute by Scheltens), was also known to Scheltens: 'he was a sergeant-major in the Guard who was nominated a lieutenant when he arrived in Paris and became a captain after Lützen'. This is true: Leboutte was a captain by June 1813.

92. The much reduced IV Corps, commanded by the viceroy of Italy, Eugene.

93. Minus 25 degrees Celsius. Vionnet uses the Reamur scale.

94. Napoleon actually left at ten that evening. Serraris wrote that, 'As we were leaving we learnt that the emperor had quit us. Discouragement.' General Roguet thought that the emperor's presence was necessary in Paris, as did Bourgogne, who thought that English agents were provoking the perhaps understandable discouragement in the army.

95. Bourgogne, now back with the unit, called it Joupranoui, but remembered it differently: 'almost all the houses had been burnt down, and the others abandoned, but they had neither roofs nor doors'.

96. General of Division D'Estrées commanded two Neapolitan brigades, whilst Loison commanded a division formed from provisional regiments. Loison, who had earned a reputation for cruelty in the Peninsular War, was later charged (without irony) by the emperor with having abandoned the army for having been absent.

97. Scheltens confirms this: 'When a horse fell down, men threw themselves on it and cut it to pieces; you would often see such an animal look round sadly as it had its hindquarters hacked into bits.'

98. Coincidentally, Bourgogne described just such an event on this day, where he and some men killed a horse for its blood (they had no axe to cut some of the meat off), and cooked it over an abandoned fire, covering their fingers and faces in blood.

99. Serraris noted that, 'The road is strewn with soldiers and horses, there are thousands of them in the snow. We no longer resemble men. Our faces are blackened by smoke, and our clothing is in shreds. Those who fall are stripped at once, even if they are still alive.'

100. Tragedy struck the regiment on the 7th of December when, according to Serraris, 'three officers and a number of soldiers from the regiment, having taken shelter in a barn along with six hundred others – generals, officers and others – were all burnt to death. I escaped as if by a miracle.' Those officers were likely to have been Major Gillet and Lieutenant Guesdon, wounded at Krasnoe, and Lieutenant Pierret, wounded at the crossing of the Beresina on the 28th of November.

101. Bourgogne says his battalion fitted into one house

previously housing men from Baden who left 'fearing we would eat them'.

102. Bourgogne and Sergeant Bailly were lucky enough to find some loaves of white bread 'as good as any in Paris'.

103. Serraris seems to have hoped that this would be the case: 'Arrival at Vilna, the Promised Land. We believed that Schwarzenberg and 150,000 Frenchmen would take our place. There was nobody. That same day [the 9th] I lost my portmanteau in a Cossack charge.'

104. Bourgogne confirms this, but he was knocked over by some fugitives and found himself with Sergeant Daubenton (and the dog, Mouton) and some Hessians waiting for the rearguard. They were scattered by some cavalry, Mouton being wounded, only to be saved by Marshal Ney and the rearguard.

105. Scheltens was one of those to benefit, whilst Bourgogne contented himself with four shirts. Many would regret attempting to carry heavy sacks containing 5 Franc pieces.

106. It was too cold to ride, as Roguet noted: 'I made the entire retreat on foot, the excessive cold meant that I could not stay on a horse. My soles were soon rendered useless and I had to protect my feet by wrapping them in rags.'

107. Prince Emile of Hesse-Darmstadt had been assigned to imperial headquarters and most of his contingent dispersed to different divisions of the army. The Guard units had formed a brigade in the Young Guard, largely destroyed at Krasnoe. The Hessians were reunited at Vilna that December, with around three hundred men escaping from Russia.

108. Roguet also lost all his servants: 'All my servants died or were taken; my wagons, correspondence, my maps, all was lost. The only thing that remained to me was the shirt on my back.' Prince Eugene lent him a coat when he reached Elbingen.

109. A few days before, Bourgogne had again become detached from the regiment, but stumbled upon a fire where the regiment was warming itself: 'Grangier recognised me and hurried over to help me with a number of my other friends. They set me down on some straw . . . Monsieur Serraris, the company lieutenant, had some brandy and he gave me a little. I then had some horsemeat soup, which was good as it had been flavoured with salt, whereas up until then we had always used gunpowder.' Bourgogne was exhausted and resolved not to leave the camp the next morning, but Serraris 'consoled me, and told me my suffering was nothing but fatigue and that I should rest in front of the fire' to continue onwards the next day, supported by Grangier and Leboude [Leboutte]. He lost the regiment again, making his way along with Sergeant Poumo and Fusilier Faloppa as far as Kovno.

110. Roguet did his best to instil some discipline. Bourgogne recalled that he saw a Chasseur of the Guard who told him, 'That foul general Roguet is using his stick to hit everyone. If he comes over here, I am waiting for him.' Roustan was also working hard: 'We were barely out of the house when I saw Adjudant-Major Roustan standing there; he recognised me and said, "Well, what are you doing there? Get out. Nobody is allowed to remain in the houses, whatever their regiment, and I have orders to beat anyone who tries to."' Colonel Bodelin ensured that none of the regiment left Kovno as a straggler, enforcing some order at the bridge over the Niemen. Some sixty men marched across. 'We saw how he was looking at the remains of his beautiful regiment, probably noting the difference to five months ago when we had crossed over that same bridge as part of an army that was so fine, and so brilliant.' The order did not last and Bourgogne found himself marching with Grangier, Leboude [Leboutte],

Oudicte [Nicolas Oudiette], Pierson and Poton, all NCOs.

111. This extended to men in his own regiment. Scheltens was wearing a green satin waistcoat under his greatcoat and this was quite thick and fringed with fur.

112. Bourgogne confirms this: 'there were many dead men who had died during the night from having drunk too much brandy or from the cold'. Scheltens too remembered a scene in which it was 'impossible to take a step without standing on the dead. Nobody has ever seen anything quite like this, or so many bodies in such a little space.'

113. After Kovno, the regiment made its own way along as best it could. Scheltens was in a group of five. Bourgogne, also straggling, approached this town with Sergeant Humblot, closely followed by Cossacks. Bourgogne, overcome by a bout of dysentery, soiled himself but still managed to flee into some woods.

114. Bourgogne was again reunited with the regiment and took part in the review. He left, with Grangier, Leboude [Leboutte], Oudicte [Oudiette] and Pierson, in a sledge.

115. Vionnet is in error here as this is a place in Brandenburg. He means Intersburg [Chernyakhovsk] between Gumbinnen and Wehlau. Serraris reached there on the 20th of December, noting that he had 'indigestion three times a day'. Bourgogne seems to think he arrived there on the 19th of December, but he is understandably confused over place names and dates by this point.

116. Bourgogne says he was here on the 18th, well before Vionnet, but Pierson crashed the sledge, causing a delay.

117. Bourgogne's sledge cost him 15 Francs, and he had arrived there on the 23rd of December. He shaved, had a bath, changed his clothes and began to feel human again. He was reviewed again, and threatened with arrest by

Roustan for having cut his queue off. The halt allowed a few stragglers to catch up, not only Vionnet, but the two Fusiliers Bourgogne saw struggling along who had been lost to the regiment since the crossing of the Beresina. They handed him a greatcoat he had entrusted them with in Moscow, in the pockets of which was a box containing five precious stones.

118. Scheltens was pleased to find gin, beer and 'even bread' here.

119. Serraris had arrived here on the 26th of December, and found waiting for him an order requiring him to return to Paris; there he was transferred to the rank of captain in the 11th Tirailleurs. Scheltens also reached the town and was incorporated into a provisional battalion of the Old Guard (all that remained of the Guard infantry), as was Sergeant Major Pierre Richard Pierson, who would be transferred to the Old Guard in March 1813. Scheltens says he would have preferred to return to Paris. Instead the unit was sent to Berlin and then Magdebourg and, later, Erfurt. He was later transferred to the 2nd Regiment of Grenadiers for the 1813 campaign. Bourgogne would be promoted into the Line, as would Sergeant Leboutte (the 145th Line), whilst Sergeant Major Nicolas Oudiette was promoted to second lieutenant in his own regiment.

120. Mayence, or Mainz, had been an archbishopric, then the Republic of Mainz, before becoming chief city of the French department of Mont-Tonerre. The ex-Jacobin Jean-Bon Saint-André, granted the title of baron, was prefect of the department in early 1813. Other inns included the Upper Town, the White Town and the City of Paris.

121. He is likely to have arrived at Rue Saint Martin.

122. Penthemont on the south bank of the Seine in Paris had

been established as an abbey in 1756 but became public property in 1790. It was a barracks for the Imperial Guard in 1813.

123. A town with a population of 6,600 in 1811, famous as a centre for manufacturing Brie.
124. A pretty and well-paved town, with a population of 3,300 in 1811.
125. Population 4,200, famous for making white soap.
126. In wine country, along the Marne. Population 2,300.
127. Famous for pink champagne in 1811 and boasting three good inns: the Ecu, the Cross of Gold and the Horse Post. Population 5,500.
128. A considerable town with a public library, a small museum of natural history, a botanical garden and an agricultural society. The Imperial Palace was a cheekily named inn, one of four recommended in contemporary guidebooks (along with the Golden Apple, the Golden Cross and the Town of Nancy).
129. The town had a population of 3,600 and had been attacked by the Prussians in 1792.
130. A town of 35,260 inhabitants, recommended inns being the Little Cross of Gold, the School of Wisdom and the Saint Louis of the Three Agreements.
131. Boasting a lead foundry and mineral waters; population 2,500.
132. A well-built town with wide streets and a population of 2,700.
133. A town with a population of 3,500.
134. Louis-Vivant Lagneau, now surgeon in the Fusiliers-Grenadiers, noted in his journal that on that day 'The battalion of the regiment commanded by Monsieur Vionnet arrived at Mayence today.'
135. Vionnet had been promoted to command the 2nd Tirailleurs of the Guard that April.

136. Frederick August I (1750–1827) ruled Saxony and, as Duke of Warsaw, some of Poland. He was to lose territory at the peace settlement in 1814–1815 for not deserting Napoleon in 1813.

137. General Pierre Lanusse (1768–1847) commanded a brigade of Guard Tirailleurs.

138. Pierre Dumoustier (1771–1831) was wounded at Dresden later that year.

139. Pierre Barrois (1774–1860) had served in Spain until 1813 and went on to fight at Waterloo, where he was wounded in the shoulder.

140. General Henri Rottembourg (1769–1857), the son of a baker, rose to command a division in 1813.

141. Géraud-Christophe-Michel Duroc (1772–1813) had been Napoleon's aide-de-camp and was appointed to this position in 1805. The roundshot hit a tree, ricocheted off and hit both General Kirgener of the Engineers and Duroc.

142. Of the 1st Regiment of Tirailleurs in the same brigade as Vionnet in Barrois's division.

143. Louis Jean François Dethan, born in 1771, had served in Spain with the 3rd Tirailleurs before becoming commander of the 2nd Battalion of the 2nd Tirailleurs. He actually died of wounds received at Leipzig in October 1813, finally succumbing on the 12th of November. Jean-Claude Vincent Guillemin commanded the other battalion; he survived to fight at Waterloo.

144. Nicolas Paillard (1756–1831) was wounded at Dresden whilst commanding a brigade of the 44th Division.

145. The castle was owned, and indeed was built, by the eccentric philanthropist Nikolai Putyatin or Putiatin. The castle, known as the Chaumière, was built in 1797 and was an eccentric Gothic creation with balconies, turrets and Romantic follies in the garden.

146. This was true for the first part of the campaign. It may

be that Michaud's earlier letters were stopped from reaching their destination – letters were being read and examined in an early form of military censorship in 1812.

147. This was Michaud's last letter. His service record ends with the remark: 'Left in the rear in Russia on the 28th of November 1812. Presumed dead.'

148. Bourgogne confirms this: 'It was three in the afternoon and we made our entry formed up in columns by platoon, the band going before. The vanguard was composed of thirty men, including myself, and Monsieur Serraris, lieutenant in our company, was in command.' The band played 'La victoire est a nous'.

149. Bourgogne remembered that 'At seven, the fire took hold behind the palace of the governor. The colonel came up and ordered that a detachment should be sent out at once. I was part of this fifteen-man patrol and Monsieur Serraris came with us and took charge.' The patrol was shot at, and the detachment came up against nine 'rascals' armed with lances and muskets. They killed them, then promptly got lost.

150. A detachment of the Regiment Joseph-Napoleon, composed of Spaniards, was based at Prince Gallitzin's palace on the outskirts of Moscow.

151. Napoleon instructed Marshal Mortier to destroy the Kremlin, writing to him on the 20th of October that 'On the 22nd or 23rd, at two o'clock in the morning, the brandy store should be set on fire, as well as the barracks and the public buildings, with the exception of the House of the Innocents. The Kremlin palace should also be set on fire. Care should be taken that all the muskets are broken into pieces, that powder should be placed in all the Kremlin's towers and that all the limbers and caisson wheels be smashed. When all this has been accomplished, and fire has taken hold of the Kremlin, the Duke of

Treviso [Mortier] should quit the Kremlin and march to Mojaisk. At four o'clock the responsible artillery officer will have the Kremlin blown up . . . Care should be taken that he himself should stay in Moscow until he sees, with his own eyes, that the Kremlin has been destroyed. Care should also be taken that the two houses belonging to the former governor and Razumovsky are also set alight.'

152. Wintzingerode was a Hessian in Russian service. He had been commanding some Russian partisans around Moscow and re-entered the capital prematurely. There he was captured by Lieutenant Leleu of the 5th Voltigeurs of the Imperial Guard: 'Being on duty in the Government Square with thirty-eight Voltigeurs of the 5th, my sentries alerted me to two officers riding towards us followed by many lancers. As I did not recognise their uniform, I approached them in order to verify who they were. The officer to the fore replied "France" when I asked "Who goes there?". As I drew closer I placed my hand on his horse's bridle and demanded of him "Who are you?" "I am a general and I have come to seize these buildings and chase out the partisans." Not believing him, I had him placed under arrest and had his suite fired upon and pursued, which was done until they were united with a larger body of cavalry of around some two hundred men. This general was accompanied by an aide-de-camp whom I also arrested, and I am sending both men to the Kremlin.' Wintzingerode was bitterly browbeaten in an interview with Napoleon, with the emperor accusing him of being from Württemberg, and therefore a Napoleonic subject, but was later liberated by partisans as he was being escorted as a prisoner towards confinement in Germany.

153. Serraris was right in this instance: it was the 1st Voltigeurs. The colonel, Mallet, was wounded and

twenty-four other officers killed or wounded. Few escaped.

154. Jacques-Marie Gillet died on the 8th of December.
155. Bourgogne probably means Captain Edme Lucotte, sent out to steady the troops. The Voltigeurs, as we have seen, were commanded by Antoine Mallet.
156. Baron Louis Longchamps commanded a brigade in Davout's I Corps, but had commanded the 1st Tirailleurs until 1811.
157. Surgeon Lagneau of the 4th Tirailleurs was 'at the first house on the right as you entered the village' and noted, as he retreated, that 'we were followed closely, and shadowed on our flanks, by Cossacks furnished with six-pounder guns mounted on planks or sledges'.
158. Napoleon had left Krasnoe at eleven o'clock on the 17th of November, spending the night at Liady until five the following morning.

Bibliography

Anon, 'Biographie du lieutenant-général messire Jean-Théodore Serraris', in *Annalen van den Oudheidskundigen Kring van het Land van Waas* (St Niklaas, 1869)

Bourgogne, Adrien, *Mémoires du sergent Bourgogne (1812–1813) publiés d'après le manuscrit original par Paul Cottin et Maurice Hénault* (Paris, 1898). First published in the *Nouvelle Revue retrospective* in 1896 (incorrectly giving Bourgogne's first names as Jean-François). Translated as *The Memoirs of Sergeant Bourgogne* (1812–1813) (London, 1899)

Deblais, Captain F., 'Un officier de la Garde impériale, lettres écrites de 1810 à 1814', in *Carnet de la Sabretache* (1926)

Fairon, Emile, and Heuse, Henri, *Lettres de Grognards* (Liège, 1936)

Lagneau, Louis-Vivant, *Journal d'un chirurgien de la Grande Armée* (Paris, 1913; repr. 2000)

Lagrave, Roger, *Joseph Vachin: enfant du Causse Méjean et soldat d'empire* (Saint-Chély-d'Apcher, 1993)

Roguet, General François, *Mémoires militaires du lieutenant général comte Roguet,* two volumes (Paris, 1862)

Scheltens, Colonel Henri, *Souvenirs d'un grenadier de la Garde* (Paris, 2005; repr. from 1880 edn)

Vionnet de Maringone, Louis Joseph, Vicomte, *Campagnes de Russie & de Saxe, 1812–1813. Souvenirs d'un ex-Commandant des Grenadiers de la Vieille-Garde. Fragments des memoires inédits du lieutenant-général L.-J. Vionnet de Maringoné. Avec preface de Rodolphe Vagnair* (Paris, 1899)

Vionnet de Maringoné, Louis Joseph, Vicomte, *Souvenirs du général Vionnet, Vicomte de Maringoné. Publiés par André Levi. Campagnes de Russie et de Saxe, 1812–1813. Insurrection de Lyon, 1816* (Paris, 1913)

In addition, Alain Le Coz has assembled a fascinating amount
of research on Vionnet's regiment at
http://www.fusiliers.lv/history/memorial

Index